QUICKBOOKS ONLINE FOR BEGINNERS

The Step-by-Step Illustrated Guide to Mastering QBO - Secret Tips to Leverage AI, Automate Tedious Tasks, Save Time and Focus on What Truly Matter

Nolan Ridge

CONTENTS

INTRODUCTION

Q uickBooks Online For Beginners is your essential guide to automating your finances, meticulously crafted to assist you in integrating this powerful tool into your business operations. With every page turn, you will discover a structured, step-by-step approach designed to not only familiarize you with QuickBooks Online but also to equip you with the skills necessary to harness its full potential.

What is exactly QuickBooks Online? It is an accounting service designed for small- to medium-sized businesses seeking to refine their financial management practices. Whether you are making the transition from manual bookkeeping or upgrading from another digital solution, this guide will lead you through every necessary process. Each chapter is carefully laid out to build upon the previous one, ensuring a comprehensive understanding of how to effectively set up, navigate, and optimize this robust software.

We begin with the basics—setting up your account and understanding the fundamental features of QuickBooks Online. As we progress, you will learn how to customize the platform to meet your unique business needs, from automating routine financial tasks to generating and analyzing reports that offer critical insights into your business's financial health.

Moreover, we'll also teach you how to apply these lessons through practical, actionable steps, showing you how to put knowledge into practice and immediately reap the benefits for your business. These segments ensure that you gain not only theoretical knowledge but also hands-on expertise, enabling you to improve your operational efficiency and financial decision-making.

It doesn't matter what stage you're at—a fledgling entrepreneur or a seasoned business owner. Our aim is to leave you with the insights and skills necessary to fully leverage QuickBooks Online, thus driving the success and growth of your business; hopefully, you'll be able to do just that by the time you reach the end of this guide.

Before we jump into the software itself, let's see why business owners strongly recommend using QuickBooks Online

Why QuickBooks is Essential for Your Business

QuickBooks has become a cornerstone in the world of small and medium-sized business finance for several compelling reasons. Using QuickBooks offers a wide array of benefits for businesses, regardless of their size or industry. From streamlining financial processes to gaining valuable insights into the company's performance, QuickBooks serves as a comprehensive solution for managing finances efficiently. QuickBooks automates repetitive accounting tasks such as invoicing, bill payments, and reconciliations. This saves time and reduces manual errors, ensuring accuracy in financial records.

In addition, QuickBooks monitors income, expenses, and cash flow in real-time with intuitive dashboards. You can gain immediate insights into the financial health of the business. It also automatically syncs bank and credit card transactions, simplifying the reconciliation process. QuickBooks can match transactions effortlessly and ensure accurate financial records. It will enable you to create customized invoices with company logos, colors, and payment terms. You can also use it to impress clients with professional-looking invoices that can be sent electronically.

With QuickBooks, you can accept online payments from customers via credit cards, ACH transfers, or online payment portals. It helps to speed up payment collections and improve cash flow.

Here are some key points illustrating why QuickBooks is essential for the success and efficiency of your business:

- **Streamlined Financial Management:** QuickBooks provides a centralized platform for managing all aspects of your company's finances. From invoicing and expense tracking to payroll and tax management, it streamlines financial tasks into one user-friendly interface.
- **Accurate Bookkeeping:** With QuickBooks, manual bookkeeping errors become a thing of the past. The software automates calculations and categorizations, reducing the likelihood of human error and ensuring accurate financial records.
- **Time Efficiency:** Time is money in business, and QuickBooks saves you both. Tasks that used to take hours can now be completed in minutes with its intuitive interface and automation features.
- **Invoicing and Payments:** Create professional-looking invoices that reflect your brand and easily send them to clients directly through QuickBooks. You can also track when invoices are viewed and paid, ensuring timely cash flow.
- **Expense Tracking and Reporting:** Keep tabs on where your money is going with detailed expense tracking. QuickBooks categorizes expenses for you, making it simple to generate reports that provide valuable insights into your spending habits.
- **Financial Insights:** QuickBooks offers a range of reports and analytics tools that give you a clear picture of your business's

financial health. Monitor profitability, cash flow, and trends to make informed decisions for growth.

- **Tax Preparation Made Easy:** QuickBooks simplifies tax time by organizing your financial data and generating accurate reports that you or your accountant can use for tax filings. This reduces stress and ensures compliance with tax regulations.

- **Scalability and Growth:** Whether you're a solopreneur or a growing enterprise, QuickBooks scales with your business. As your needs evolve, you can easily upgrade to more advanced versions with additional features to support your growth.

- **Improved Cash Flow Management:** By tracking your receivables and payables in real-time, QuickBooks helps you optimize your cash flow. Know when to expect payments and plan your expenses accordingly to maintain a healthy financial position.

- **Integration with Third-Party Apps:** QuickBooks integrates seamlessly with a wide range of third-party apps and services. Whether you need project management tools, e-commerce platforms, or CRM software, you can sync them with QuickBooks for a fully integrated business solution.

- **Enhanced Collaboration:** If you have an accountant or bookkeeper, QuickBooks makes collaboration easy. You can grant access to specific areas of your financial data, allowing them to work remotely and efficiently with up-to-date information.

- **Compliance and Audit Trail:** QuickBooks helps you stay compliant with financial regulations by providing audit trails and ensuring all transactions are recorded accurately. This gives you peace of mind during audits or regulatory reviews.

This informative eBook will focus on a series of topics that can enable the reader to better understand QuickBooks and how beneficial it can be to a business enterprise. Some of the topics that will be discussed are highlighted below:

- Getting Started with QuickBooks
- Basic Operations in QuickBooks Online
- Managing Sales and Income
- Expenses and Vendors
- Payroll and Employees
- And many more

The information provided in this eBook is simplified to make it very easy for all categories of readers to understand and seamlessly apply them in real life.

YOUR OPINION MATTERS!

Your feedback is crucial—not only to me but also to future readers who, like you, seek a reliable guidance.

If you could take a few moments to write a review, it would mean the world to me!! Your honest thoughts and insights are invaluable in helping me improve and ensuring I continue to meet your needs.

Scan me!

Thank you for your review and for helping me grow.
Your support is truly appreciated.

With gratitude,
Nolan Ridge

CHAPTER 1
GETTING STARTED WITH QUICKBOOKS

Welcome to QuickBooks Online: Your Financial Management Solution

What is QuickBooks Online?

QuickBooks Online is a cloud-based accounting software developed by Intuit. It's designed to help small and medium-sized businesses manage their finances efficiently. QuickBooks Online offers a range of features to help users track income and expenses, create and send invoices, manage bills and payments, run financial reports, and more.

Features and Capabilities

QuickBooks Online is a robust accounting software that offers a wide range of features and capabilities to help businesses manage their finances effectively. Here are some of the key features and capabilities of QuickBooks Online:

- **Dashboard Overview:** The dashboard provides a snapshot of your business's financial health, displaying key metrics like profit and loss, expenses, sales, and bank account balances.
- **Income and Expense Tracking:** Categorize and track income and expenses automatically by connecting bank and credit card accounts. Create rules to categorize transactions for quicker reconciliation.
- **Invoicing:** Customize and create professional invoices with your company logo. Send invoices to customers via email and track when they are viewed and paid. Accept online payments from customers through various payment gateways like credit cards and ACH bank transfers.
- **Expense Management:** Capture and categorize expenses by uploading receipts and attaching them to transactions. Track and manage vendor bills, set up recurring payments, and get reminders for due dates.
- **Bank Reconciliation:** Automatically download and categorize bank transactions, making reconciliation faster and more accurate. Match transactions with existing entries to avoid duplicates and errors.
- **Financial Reporting:** Generate a variety of financial reports such as profit and loss, balance sheet, cash flow statement, and customizable reports. Access real-time insights into your business's performance to make informed decisions.
- **Sales and Sales Tax:** Track sales and sales tax, including creating and managing sales receipts and estimates. Automatically calculate and track sales tax liabilities based on your location and tax rules.
- **Inventory Management:** Track and manage inventory levels, set re-order points, and get notified when stock is low. Sync inventory data with sales orders and invoices to maintain accurate records.

- **Time Tracking:** Track billable hours for projects and clients. Generate timesheets, bill customers for time worked, and analyze profitability by project.
- **Payroll (Additional Service):** Integrate with QuickBooks Online Payroll for easy payroll processing. Calculate paychecks, withholdings, and taxes automatically. File payroll taxes and generate W-2s for employees.
- **Multi-User Access and Collaboration:** Invite your accountant or team members to collaborate and access the same data in real-time. Assign roles and permissions to control what users can see and do.
- **Mobile App:** Access QuickBooks Online on-the-go with the mobile app (available for iOS and Android). Create invoices, capture receipts, view reports, and manage finances from your smartphone or tablet.
- **Integration Ecosystem:** QuickBooks Online integrates with a wide range of third-party apps and services, such as payment processors, CRM systems, e-commerce platforms, and more. Sync data seamlessly across different tools to streamline workflows and improve efficiency.

Why Choose QuickBooks Online?

There are several reasons why businesses choose QuickBooks Online as their accounting software solution. Here are some of the key benefits and reasons to consider using QuickBooks Online:

1. Accessibility and Convenience:

- **Cloud-Based:** QuickBooks Online is a cloud-based accounting software, meaning you can access it from anywhere with an internet connection. This allows business owners, accountants, and employees to work remotely or on-the-go.
- **Mobile App:** The mobile app lets you manage your finances, send invoices, capture receipts, and view reports from your smartphone or tablet.

2. Ease of Use:

- QuickBooks Online is designed with a user-friendly interface, making it accessible even to those without an accounting background.
- Intuitive navigation and clear instructions make it easy to set up and start using the software quickly.

3. Time-Saving Features:

- **Automation:** Many repetitive tasks such as invoicing, expense tracking, and bank reconciliation can be automated, saving you time and reducing errors.
- **Bank Integration:** Connect your bank and credit card accounts to automatically import transactions, making reconciliation faster and more accurate.

4. Financial Management:

- **Real-Time Data:** Get up-to-date insights into your business's financial health with real-time data and reports.
- **Customizable Reports:** Generate a variety of customizable reports to analyze performance, cash flow, profitability, and more.

5. Invoicing and Payment Processing:

- Create and customize professional invoices with your logo and branding.
- Send invoices directly to customers via email and track when they are viewed and paid.
- Accept online payments from customers through various payment gateways, improving cash flow.

6. Expense Tracking and Management:

- Easily track and categorize expenses by uploading receipts or linking accounts.

- Manage vendor bills, set up recurring payments, and get reminders for due dates.

7. Tax Preparation and Compliance:

- QuickBooks Online helps simplify tax preparation by organizing your financial data.
- Automatically calculate and track sales tax, making it easier to file taxes accurately and on time.
- Generate reports and data that are useful for tax filing purposes.

8. Scalability and Customization:

- QuickBooks Online offers different plans to suit the needs of businesses of all sizes.
- As your business grows, you can easily upgrade your plan to access more features and capabilities.
- Customize invoices, reports, and workflows to match your business's specific needs.

9. Integration Ecosystem:

- QuickBooks Online integrates with a wide range of third-party apps and services, such as payment processors, CRM systems, e-commerce platforms, and more.
- Sync data seamlessly across different tools to streamline workflows and improve efficiency.

10. Security and Data Protection:

- QuickBooks Online uses advanced encryption and security measures to protect your financial data.
- Regular backups ensure that your data is safe and secure, minimizing the risk of data loss.

11. Customer Support and Training:

- Access to customer support via phone, chat, or email to help with any questions or issues.
- Extensive online resources, tutorials, and training materials to learn how to use the software effectively.

12. Affordability:

- QuickBooks Online offers various pricing plans to fit different budgets and business needs.
- Subscription-based pricing means you can pay monthly or annually without the need for a large upfront investment.

CHAPTER 2
BASIC OPERATIONS IN QUICKBOOKS ONLINE

Recording Transactions: Sales, Expenses, and Payments

Understanding Transaction Types

Understanding different transaction types is essential for proper accounting and financial management. Here are some common transaction types that you might encounter in your business, along with explanations of each:

1. Sales Transactions:

- **Sales Receipts:** These are created when a customer pays you at the time of sale. It records the income immediately.
- **Invoices:** Created when you sell products or services to customers on credit. The invoice records the sale and indicates that payment is expected at a later date.

2. Expense Transactions:

- **Vendor Bills:** These are records of money your business owes to vendors for goods or services purchased on credit. Bills indicate that you owe payment at a later date.
- **Expense Transactions:** Direct expenses incurred by your business, such as rent, utilities, office supplies, and salaries.

3. Banking Transactions:

- **Deposits:** Money coming into your bank account, including customer payments, loans, and transfers from other accounts.
- **Withdrawals:** Money leaving your bank account, such as payments to vendors, employee payroll, and owner withdrawals.

4. Asset Transactions:

- **Asset Purchases:** Buying fixed assets for your business, such as equipment, vehicles, or property.
- **Depreciation:** Represents the gradual decrease in the value of assets over time. Depreciation expenses are recorded to reflect this decrease.

5. Liability Transactions:

- **Loan Payments:** Repayments made towards business loans or lines of credit.
- **Credit Card Payments:** Payments made towards credit card balances used for business expenses.

6. Equity Transactions:

- **Owner Contributions:** When the owner puts personal funds into the business.
- **Owner Withdrawals/Distributions:** When the owner takes money out of the business for personal use.

7. Inventory Transactions:

- **Inventory Purchases:** When you purchase inventory items for resale.
- **Inventory Sales:** When you sell inventory items to customers.

8. Payroll Transactions:

- **Employee Payroll:** Payments made to employees for their work.
- **Payroll Taxes:** Taxes withheld from employee paychecks, such as income tax, Social Security, and Medicare.
- **Employer Payroll Taxes:** Taxes paid by the employer on behalf of employees, such as unemployment tax and Social Security contributions.

9. Adjusting Entries:

- **Accruals:** Entries made to record revenues or expenses that have been earned or incurred but not yet recorded.
- **Deferrals:** Entries made to defer the recognition of revenues or expenses to a future period.

10. Intercompany Transactions:

- Transactions between different entities or departments within the same company.

11. Miscellaneous Transactions:

- **Contra Entries:** Entries that offset each other, such as reversing entries.
- **Journal Entries:** Manual entries used to adjust account balances, correct errors, or record unique transactions not covered by other transaction types.

12. Transfer Transactions:

- **Account Transfers**: Movements of money between different accounts within the same financial institution. This is used to manage cash flow effectively across various business accounts.

- **Interbank Transfers**: Transfers between accounts held at different banks or financial institutions. These are crucial for businesses managing multiple banking relationships.

- **Electronic Fund Transfers (EFT)**: Digital transfers of money from one bank account to another, either within the same bank or between different banks. EFTs are used for vendor payments, bill payments, and payroll.

- **Wire Transfers**: Immediate, same-day transfers of funds across banks, typically used for large, time-sensitive payments domestically or internationally.

Entering Sales Transactions

Entering sales transactions in QuickBooks Online is a fundamental task for recording your business's revenue accurately. Here's a step-by-step guide on how to enter sales transactions such as sales receipts and invoices in QuickBooks Online:

1. Accessing the Sales Transactions: Log in to your QuickBooks Online account.

2. Navigate to the Sales Menu: From the left-hand menu, click on "Sales" and "All Sales" or "Sales" in the top navigation bar.

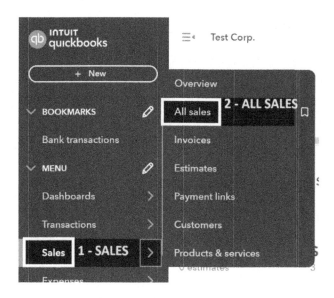

3. Entering a Sales Receipt: Click on "New Transaction" and then click on "Sales Receipt" or "Create Sales Receipt" (depending on your version).

Fill out the required fields:

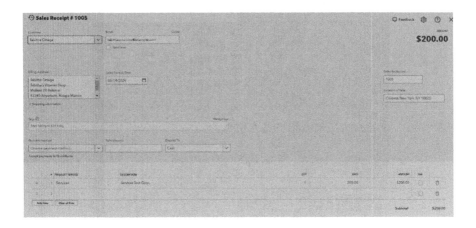

- **Customer:** Select the customer from the drop-down menu.
- **Date:** Enter the date of the sale.
- **Product/Service:** Choose the product or service sold from the drop-down list.
- **Description:** Add a description if needed.
- **Payment Method:** Select the payment method.
- **Deposit to:** Choose the bank account where the funds will be deposited.
- **Quantity:** Enter the quantity sold. (on Add lines row)
- **Rate:** Enter the price per unit. (on Add lines row)
- **Save and Close:** Once all information is entered, click "Save and Close" to record the sales receipt.

4. Entering an Invoice:

Click on "New Invoice" or "Create Invoice" or "New Transaction" →
"Invoice" (depending on your version).

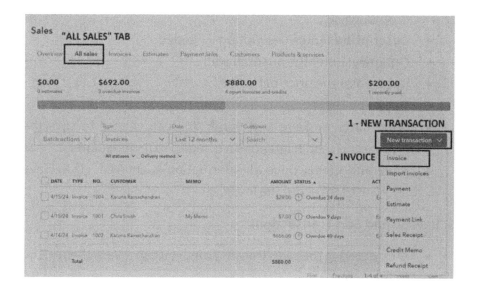

Fill out the required fields:

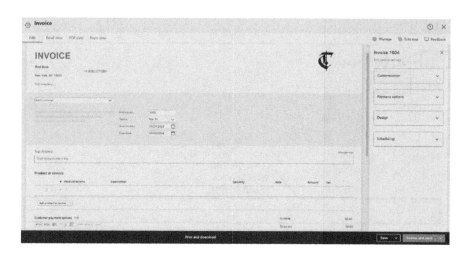

- **Customer:** Select the customer from the drop-down menu.
- **Invoice Date:** Enter the date of the invoice.
- **Due Date:** Enter the date by which payment is due.
- **Product/Service:** Choose the product or service sold from the drop-down list.
- **Description:** Add a description if needed.
- **Quantity:** Enter the quantity sold.
- **Rate:** Enter the price per unit.
- **Payment Terms:** Select the payment terms (e.g., Net 30).
- **Send Later or Save and Send:** You can choose to save the invoice and send it later or save and send it immediately.
- **Save and Close:** Once all information is entered, click "Save and Close" to record the invoice.

5. Review and Edit Transactions:

- After entering the sales transactions, you can review them in the Sales menu.
- To edit a transaction, find it in the list, click on it to open, make changes, and then save the changes.

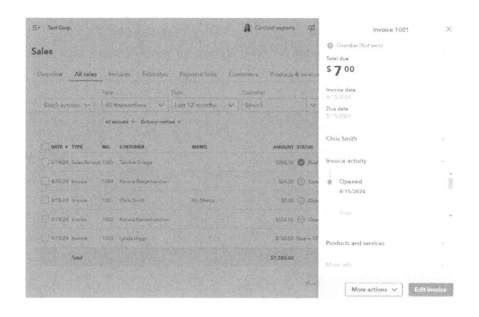

6. Recording Payments Received:

- When a customer pays an invoice, you'll need to record the payment.
- Go to the Sales menu and select "Receive Payment."

- Select the customer and the invoice that was paid.
- Enter the payment amount, payment method, and any other required details.

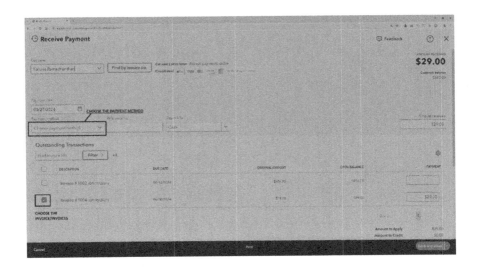

- Click "Save and Close" to record the payment.

7. Viewing Reports:

- QuickBooks Online offers various reports that can help you track sales, outstanding invoices, customer balances, and more.
- Go to the Reports menu to access these reports and customize them as needed.

Tips:

- Customize invoices and sales receipts with your company logo and branding for a professional look.
- Set up recurring invoices for regular customers to save time.
- Utilize payment reminders and overdue notices to encourage timely payments from customers.
- Make use of QuickBooks Online's integration with payment processors to accept online payments.

Managing Expenses and Bills

Managing expenses and bills in QuickBooks Online is crucial for maintaining accurate financial records and tracking your business's spending. Here's a step-by-step guide on how to manage expenses and bills in QuickBooks Online:

1. Entering Expenses:

From the left-hand menu, click on "Expenses" or "Expenses" in the top navigation bar.

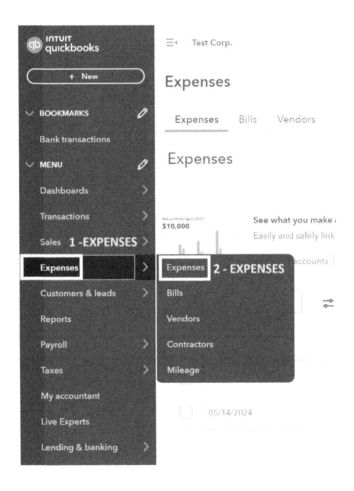

A. Enter a New Expense:

- Click on "New Expense" or "New Expense" or "New Transaction" → "Expense" (depending on your version).

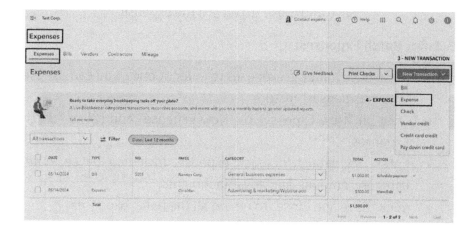

- Fill out the required fields:

- o **Payee:** Select the vendor or payee from the drop-down menu.
- o **Payment Date:** Enter the date of the expense.
- o **Category:** Choose the appropriate expense account from the drop-down list.
- o **Payment Method:** Select the payment method.

> o **Amount:** Enter the amount of the expense.
> o **Attachment:** Upload a receipt or document related to the expense (optional).
> o **Save and Close:** Once all information is entered, click "Save and Close" to record the expense.

B. Enter Batch Expenses:

- If you have multiple expenses to enter at once, you can use the "Batch Expenses" feature.
- Click on "New Expense" or "New Expense" and select "Batch Expenses."
- Enter the details for each expense, including payee, date, category, amount, and any attachments.
- Click "Save and Close" to record all the batch expenses.

2. Managing Bills:

Bills are expenses that you've received but haven't paid yet. Managing bills helps you keep track of what you owe to vendors.

A. Enter a New Bill:

- From the left-hand menu, click on "Expenses" or "Expenses" in the top navigation bar.
- Click on "New Transaction" and then click on "Bill" or click on "New Expense" (depending on your version).

- **Fill out the required fields:**
  - **Vendor:** Choose the vendor from the drop-down menu.
  - **Bill Date:** Enter the date of the bill.
  - **Due Date:** Enter the due date for payment.
  - **Category:** Select the appropriate expense account.
  - **Amount:** Enter the total amount of the bill.
  - **Save and Close:** Once all information is entered, click "Save and Close" to record the bill.

B. Manage Existing Bills:

- To view or manage existing bills, go to the "Expenses" or "Expenses" menu and select "Bills."
- Here, you can see a list of all your bills, their due dates, and amounts owed.
- Click on a bill to open it, make changes if needed, and then save the changes.
- To mark a bill as paid, click on "Make Payment" and enter the payment details.

3. Recording Bill Payments:

When it's time to pay a bill, you'll need to record the payment in QuickBooks Online.

A. Record Bill Payment:

Go to the "Expenses" or "Expenses" menu and select "Bill" tab and then select "Pay Bills".

- Choose the bill(s) you want to pay from the list.

- Enter the payment date, payment method, and amount paid for each bill.
- Click "Save and Close" to record the bill payment.

4. Reviewing Expenses and Bills:

- QuickBooks Online provides various reports to help you track and review your expenses and bills.
- Go to the "Reports" menu and select "Expenses and Purchases" or "Vendors and Payables" to access these reports.
- Customize reports based on date ranges, vendors, categories, and more.

Processing Payments

Processing payments in QuickBooks Online is a crucial step to record when customers pay invoices or bills are paid to vendors. Here's a guide on how to process payments for invoices and bills in QuickBooks Online:

Processing Customer Payments for Invoices:

1. Navigate to the Sales Menu:

- From the left-hand menu, click on "Sales" or "Invoicing" in the top navigation bar.

2. View Open Invoices:

- Click on "Invoices" to view a list of open invoices awaiting payment.

3. Select an Invoice to Record Payment:

- Click on the invoice that you want to record payment for.

4. Record Payment:

- On the invoice page, you'll see an option to "Receive Payment" or "Record Payment." Click on it.

5. Enter Payment Details:

- **Payment Date:** Date when the payment was received.
- **Payment Method:** Choose the payment method (cash, check, credit card, etc.).
- **Reference No./Check No.:** If applicable, enter a reference or check number.
- **Amount Received:** Enter the amount received from the customer.
- **Deposit To:** Select the bank account where the payment will be deposited.
- **Save and Close:** Click "Save and Close" to record the payment.

6. Review Payment:

- QuickBooks will mark the invoice as paid, and the payment will be recorded in the system.
- You can view the updated status of the invoice in the "Sales" menu under "Invoices."

Processing Vendor Payments for Bills:

1. Navigate to the Expenses Menu:

- From the left-hand menu, click on "Expenses" or "Expenses" in the top navigation bar.

2. View Open Bills:

- Click on "Bills" to view a list of open bills awaiting payment.

3. Select a Bill to Record Payment:

- Click on the bill that you want to record payment for.

4. Record Payment:

- On the bill page, you'll see an option to "Make Payment" or "Record Payment." Click on it.

5. Enter Payment Details:

- **Payment Date:** Date when the payment was made.
- **Payment Method:** Choose the payment method (check, credit card, bank transfer, etc.).
- **Reference No./Check No.:** If applicable, enter a reference or check number.
- **Amount Paid:** Enter the amount paid to the vendor.
- **Account:** Select the bank account from which the payment is made.
- **Save and Close:** Click "Save and Close" to record the payment.

6. Review Payment:

- QuickBooks will mark the bill as paid, and the payment will be recorded in the system.

- You can view the updated status of the bill in the "Expenses" menu under "Bills."

Managing Your Chart of Accounts

Introduction to Chart of Accounts

The Chart of Accounts in QuickBooks Online is a foundational part of your accounting system. It is a comprehensive list of all the accounts used by your business to record financial transactions. Each account represents a specific type of transaction, asset, liability, equity, revenue, or expense.

Purpose of Chart of Accounts

The primary purpose of the Chart of Accounts is to organize financial transactions and facilitate the recording, tracking, and reporting of a company's financial activities. It provides a structured framework for classifying transactions into categories, making it easier to generate financial statements, analyze data, and make informed business decisions.

The Chart of Accounts helps you:

- **Classify Transactions:** Each account is assigned a specific category, making it easier to classify and organize transactions.
- **Generate Financial Statements:** The Chart of Accounts forms the basis for generating key financial statements such as the balance sheet, income statement, and cash flow statement.
- **Track Income and Expenses:** It allows you to track your business's income, expenses, assets, liabilities, and equity in an organized manner.

- **Facilitate Decision-Making:** By providing a clear overview of your financial position, the Chart of Accounts helps in making informed business decisions.

Components of Chart of Accounts

The Chart of Accounts typically consists of five main types of accounts:

Assets (Accounts 1000 - 1999):

- Assets are resources owned by the company that provide future economic benefits.
- Examples include cash, accounts receivable, inventory, property, equipment, and investments.

Liabilities (Accounts 2000 - 2999):

- Liabilities are obligations or debts owed by the company to external parties.
- Examples include accounts payable, loans payable, accrued expenses, and deferred revenue.

Equity (Accounts 3000 - 3999):

- Equity represents the ownership interest in the company, including capital invested by owners and retained earnings.
- Examples include owner's equity, common stock, and retained earnings.

Income or Revenue (Accounts 4000 - 4999):

- Income accounts record money earned from sales of goods or services.

- Examples include sales revenue, service revenue, interest income, and rental income.

Expenses (Accounts 5000 - 9999):

- Expense accounts represent costs incurred in the operation of the business.
- Examples include rent, utilities, salaries, cost of goods sold, advertising, and depreciation.

Example Accounts in Chart of Accounts

Here's a simplified example of how accounts might be categorized in a Chart of Accounts:

Assets:

- 1010 - Cash
- 1020 - Accounts Receivable
- 1030 - Inventory
- 1040 - Prepaid Expenses

Liabilities:

- 2010 - Accounts Payable
- 2020 - Loans Payable
- 2030 - Accrued Expenses

Equity:

- 3010 - Owner's Capital
- 3020 - Retained Earnings

Income:

- 4010 - Sales Revenue
- 4020 - Service Revenue
- 4030 - Interest Income

Expenses:

- 5010 - Rent Expense
- 5020 - Utilities Expense
- 5030 - Salaries Expense
- 5040 - Advertising Expense

Benefits of a Well-Structured Chart of Accounts

- **Accurate Financial Reporting:** Enables the preparation of financial statements such as the balance sheet, income statement, and cash flow statement.
- **Efficient Bookkeeping:** Streamlines the recording and tracking of transactions, ensuring consistency and accuracy.
- **Facilitates Analysis:** Provides insights into business performance, trends, and areas of improvement.
- **Supports Decision-Making:** Helps management make informed decisions based on financial data.
- **Compliance:** Ensures compliance with accounting standards and tax regulations.

Setting Up Your Chart of Accounts

Setting up your Chart of Accounts in QuickBooks Online is a crucial step in organizing and categorizing your business's financial transactions. Here's a step-by-step guide on how to set up your Chart of Accounts:

1. Accessing the Chart of Accounts:

- Log in to your QuickBooks Online account.
- From the left-hand menu, go to "Transaction" or "Settings" and select "Chart of Accounts."

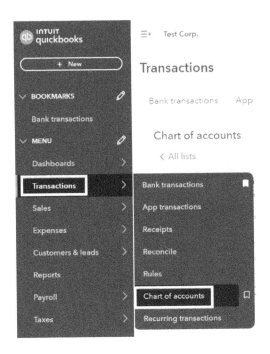

or

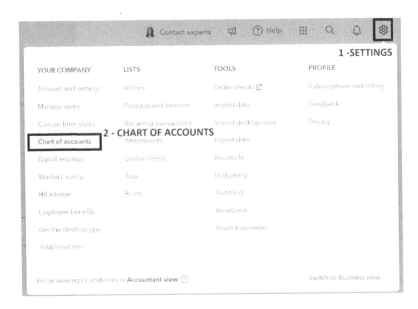

2. Default Accounts:

- QuickBooks Online provides a default Chart of Accounts based on your industry. You can choose to use this as a starting point and customize it as needed.
- To add a new account, click on the "New" button in the upper-right corner.

3. Adding New Accounts:

Click on "New" to create a new account. Select the appropriate account type from the dropdown menu (e.g., Bank, Expense, Income, etc.).

Enter the details for the new account:

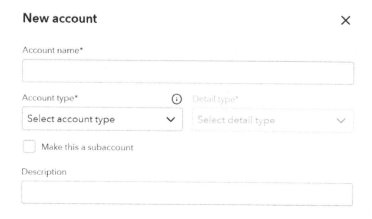

- **Name:** Enter a descriptive name for the account (e.g., "Checking Account," "Rent Expense," "Sales Revenue," etc.).
- **Detail Type:** Choose the specific category or detail type that best fits the account (e.g., "Bank," "Advertising Expense," "Sales of Product Income," etc.).

- **Description:** Optionally, you can add a description to provide more information about the account.
- **Sub-Account:** If this account is a sub-account of another account, you can select the parent account from the dropdown menu.
- **Save and Close:** Once all details are entered, click "Save and Close" to add the new account to your Chart of Accounts.

4. Editing Accounts:

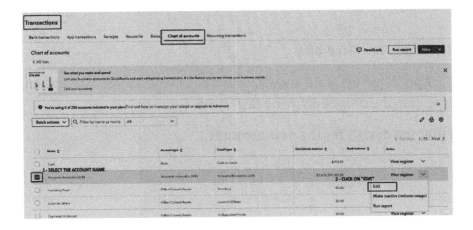

- To edit an existing account, find it in the Chart of Accounts list and click on it to open.
- Make the necessary changes to the account name, detail type, description, etc.
- Click "Save and Close" to save the changes.

5. Deleting Accounts:

- If you need to delete an account, find it in the Chart of Accounts list and click on it to open.
- Click on the "Delete" button in the bottom-left corner.
- Confirm the deletion when prompted.

6. Reordering Accounts:

- You can change the order of accounts in the Chart of Accounts by dragging and dropping them into the desired position.
- Simply click on an account and drag it to the desired location within the list.

7. Setting Opening Balances:

- If you are starting to use QuickBooks Online partway through the year, you may need to enter opening balances for your accounts.
- Go to "Transaction" > "Chart of Accounts" and click on the account for which you want to enter an opening balance.
- Click on the "Edit" button and enter the opening balance amount and date.
- Save the changes.

8. Customizing Account Numbers:

- QuickBooks Online allows you to assign account numbers to your accounts for easier organization and reference.
- Go to the "Gear" icon at top right select "Company settings" > Advanced > Chart of accounts > Enable account numbers.

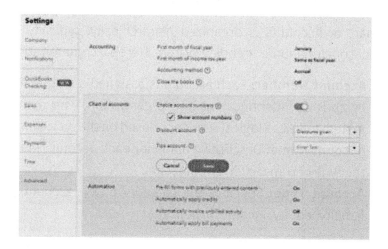

- Assign numbers to your accounts based on your preferred numbering system.
- Save the changes.

9. Review and Customize Categories:

- Review the default account categories provided by QuickBooks Online.
- Customize categories to match your specific business needs, such as adding new expense categories, income categories, etc.

10. Managing Sub-Accounts:

- Create sub-accounts to provide more detailed breakdowns of your main accounts.
- For example, you can have "Rent Expense" as a main account, with sub-accounts for "Office Rent" and "Warehouse Rent."

11. Saving and Applying Changes:

- Make sure to click "Save and Close" after adding, editing, or deleting accounts to apply the changes to your Chart of Accounts.

Organizing the Chart of Accounts

The Chart of Accounts is organized hierarchically, typically with a numerical or alphanumeric coding system. Here's a common structure:

- **Account Number:** Each account is assigned a unique number or code for identification and organization. The numbering system follows a logical sequence based on the type of account.
- **Account Name:** Descriptive name for each account, indicating the type of transaction it represents.
- **Account Type:** Specifies the category of the account (asset, liability, equity, income, expense).

- **Sub-Accounts:** Additional levels of detail can be added through sub-accounts. For example, under "Utilities Expense," you might have sub-accounts for "Electricity," "Water," "Gas," etc.

Customizing the Chart of Accounts

In QuickBooks Online, you have the flexibility to customize and tailor your Chart of Accounts to suit your business's specific needs. Here's how you can customize it:

- **Adding Accounts:** Create new accounts to track different types of transactions specific to your business.
- **Editing Accounts:** Modify existing account names, descriptions, or types to better reflect your business operations.
- **Deleting or Hiding Accounts:** Remove accounts that are no longer needed or hide inactive accounts from view.
- **Setting Account Numbers:** Assign numerical codes to accounts for easier organization and reference.

Using Sub-Accounts

Sub-accounts allow you to create a hierarchy within your Chart of Accounts. This can be useful for tracking detailed expenses or income categories under broader headings. For example:

- **Main Account:** Rent Expense
- **Sub-Accounts:** Office Rent, Warehouse Rent

Setting Up Opening Balances

If you are starting to use QuickBooks Online partway through the fiscal year, you'll need to enter opening balances for your accounts. This ensures that your financial statements accurately reflect your business's financial position.

CHAPTER 3
MANAGING SALES AND INCOME

Creating Invoices and Sales Receipts

Introduction and Set Up for Sales Documents

Sales documents in QuickBooks Online, such as invoices and sales receipts, are essential for recording your business's sales transactions and keeping track of customer payments. Here's an introduction and step-by-step guide on how to set up and use sales documents in QuickBooks Online:

1. Introduction to Sales Documents:

- **Invoices:** An invoice is a request for payment sent to customers for goods or services provided. It includes details such as the items sold, quantities, prices, terms, and payment due dates.
- **Sales Receipts:** A sales receipt is a record of a sale that has been completed and paid for immediately. It is used for transactions where payment is received at the time of sale.

2. Setting Up Sales Documents:

Before you create sales documents, ensure your products and services are set up in QuickBooks Online. You can add items by going to "Sales" > "Products and Services" > "New."

3. Creating an Invoice:

From the left-hand menu, go to "All sales" tab and click "New Transaction" and then click "Invoice" or go to "Sales", select "Invoices" and then click on "New Invoice" or "Create Invoice" (depending on your version).

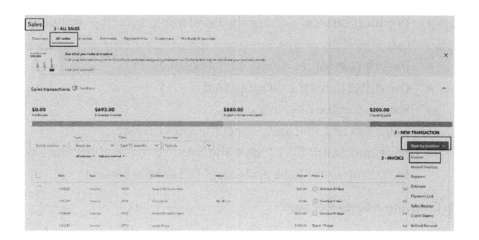

Fill out the required fields:

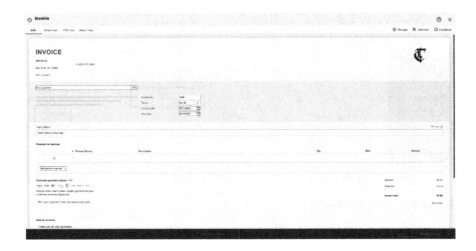

- **Customer:** Select the customer from the dropdown list.
- **Invoice Date:** Enter the date of the invoice.
- **Due Date:** Enter the date by which payment is due.
- **Product/Service:** Choose the item(s) sold from the dropdown list.
- **Description:** Add a description if needed.
- **Quantity:** Enter the quantity sold.
- **Rate:** Enter the price per unit.
- **Sales Tax:** If applicable, select the sales tax rate.
- **Save and Send:** Click "Save and Send" to email the invoice to the customer or "Save and Close" to save the invoice.

4. Creating a Sales Receipt:

Go to "All sales" and click "New Transaction" and then click "Sales Receipts" or go to "Sales", select "Sales Receipts" and then click on "New Invoice" or "Create Invoice" (depending on your version).

Fill out the required fields:

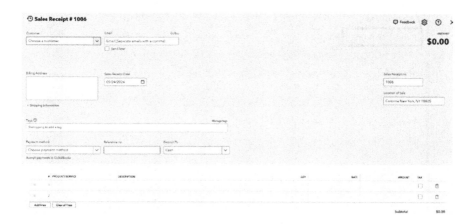

- **Customer:** Select the customer from the dropdown list.
- **Sales Receipt Date:** Enter the date of the sale.
- **Product/Service:** Choose the item(s) sold from the dropdown list.
- **Description:** Add a description if needed.
- **Payment Method:** Select the payment method (e.g., cash, credit card).
- **Deposit To:** Choose the bank account where the funds will be deposited.
- **Save and Close:** Click "Save and Close" to record the sales receipt.

5. Customizing Sales Forms:

- QuickBooks Online allows you to customize the look and feel of your sales forms, such as invoices and sales receipts.
- Go to "Settings" > "Account settings"

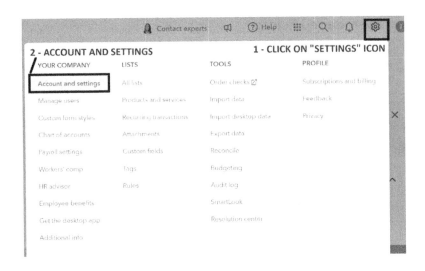

- Go to "Sales" > "Customize look and feel"

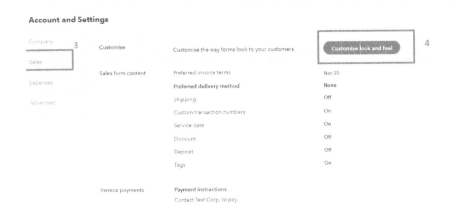

- And finally click "Edit"

6. Managing Sales Documents:

- You can view and manage all your sales documents in the "Sales" or "Invoicing" menu.
- To view, edit, or delete an invoice or sales receipt, click on the respective transaction in the list.

7. Recording Customer Payments:

- When a customer makes a payment, you'll need to record it in QuickBooks Online.
- Go to "Sales" > "Customers" > select the customer.
- Click on "Receive Payment" and fill out the payment details.
- Match the payment to the corresponding invoice or sales receipt.

8. Generating Reports:

- QuickBooks Online offers various reports related to sales, such as sales by customer, sales by product, and open invoices.
- Go to the "Reports" menu and select "Sales and Customers" to access these reports.

Creating an Invoice

Creating an invoice in QuickBooks Online is a straightforward process. Here's a step-by-step guide on how to create an invoice:

Steps to Create an Invoice

1. Accessing the Invoices Section:

- Log in to your QuickBooks Online account.
- From the left-hand menu, go to "Sales" or "Invoicing" and select "Invoices" or "All Sales" (depending on your version)

2. Start a New Invoice:

- Click on the "New Transaction" and click "Invoice"; or click on S button (depending on your version)

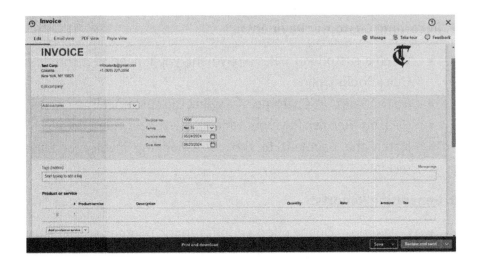

3. Fill Out Customer Details:

- Select the customer from the "Customer" dropdown menu.
- If the customer is not listed, you can click on "Add new" to create a new customer profile.

4. Enter Invoice Details:

- **Invoice Date:** Enter the date of the invoice.
- **Due Date:** QuickBooks will automatically populate this based on your payment terms, but you can adjust it if needed.
- **Invoice Number:** QuickBooks will automatically assign an invoice number, but you can change it if needed.
- **PO Number (Optional):** Enter a purchase order number if applicable

5. Add Line Items:

- Under "Product/Service," select the item(s) you are invoicing for from the dropdown menu.
- If the item is not listed, you can click on "Add new" to create a new product or service.
- Enter the quantity and rate for each item.
- QuickBooks will automatically calculate the total amount for each line item.

6. Include Additional Details (Optional):

- **Description:** Add a description for each line item if needed.
- **Sales Tax:** If applicable, select the appropriate sales tax rate for the invoice.

7. Customize Invoice Settings (Optional):

- Click on the "Customize" button to customize the appearance of your invoice.
- You can add a logo, change colors, add custom fields, and more.

8. Preview and Save:

- Click on the "Preview" button to review the invoice.
- Make sure all details are accurate.
- Click "Save and Close" to save the invoice.

9. Send the Invoice:

After saving the invoice, you have the option to send it to your customer:

- **Email:** Click on "Save and Send" to email the invoice directly from QuickBooks.
- **Print or Download:** Click on the "Print" or "Download" button to print or save a PDF copy of the invoice.

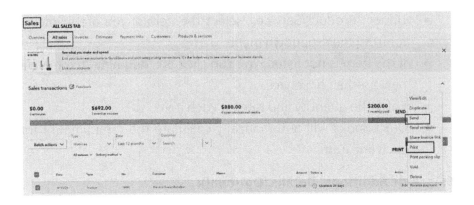

Tips for Creating Invoices in QuickBooks Online

- **Set Default Terms:** Go to "Settings" > "Account and Settings" > "Sales" to set default payment terms for your invoices.
- **Use Item Details:** Add detailed descriptions to your products and services in the "Products and Services" list for clarity on invoices.
- **Recurring Invoices:** For recurring billing, set up recurring invoices to save time. Go to "Sales" > "Recurring Transactions" to create a new recurring invoice.
- **Track Invoice Status:** Monitor the status of your invoices in QuickBooks. Open the invoice list to view which ones are open, paid, or overdue.
- **Accept Online Payments:** Enable online payment options for your customers by integrating payment gateways like PayPal or Stripe.
- **Attach Files:** You can attach files such as contracts or receipts to invoices for customer reference.

Optimizing the Invoice Payment Process

Optimizing the invoice payment process in QuickBooks can streamline your accounts receivable, improve cash flow, and enhance overall efficiency. Here are steps to help you optimize the invoice payment process within QuickBooks:

Step 1: Set Up QuickBooks for Efficient Invoicing

- **Customize Invoice Templates**:

- Go to the "Gear" icon > "All Lists" > "Custom form Style"

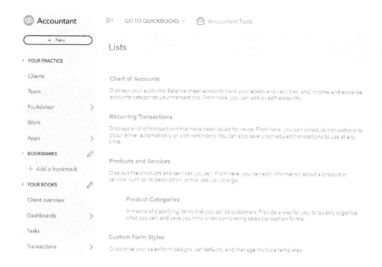

Or

- Go to "+" sign > Invoice > "customize"

Step 2: Enable Online Payments

- **Set up QuickBooks Payments:**
  - From the "Customers & leads" menu, select "Customers", then select "Receive Payment" to set up payment options.

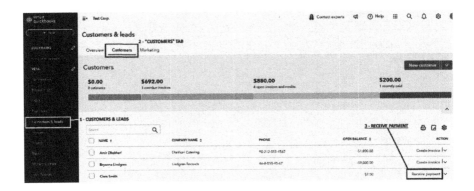

  - Choose to set up QuickBooks Payments to accept credit card payments and ACH transfers directly on invoices.

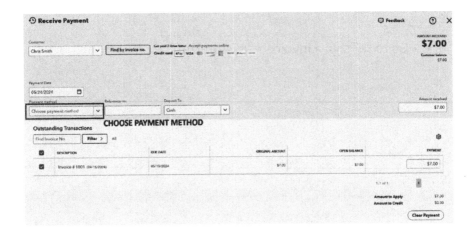

  - Follow the prompts to connect your bank account and verify your details for transactions.

Step 3: Automate Invoice Creation and Sending

- **Schedule Recurring Invoices:**
  - Navigate to Sales Tab: Log in to your QuickBooks Online account and click on the "Sales" tab in the left-hand navigation menu.
  - Select Recurring Transactions: Within the Sales tab, click on "Recurring Transactions."
  - Create New Recurring Invoice: Look for the "New Recurring Transaction" button, usually located at the top-right corner of the Recurring Transactions page, and click on it.
  - Choose Invoice: From the dropdown menu, select "Invoice" as the type of recurring transaction you want to create.
  - Fill in Invoice Details: Enter all the necessary details for the invoice, including customer information, items/services sold, quantities, prices, and any other relevant information.
  - Set Recurrence Schedule: Below the invoice details, specify how often you want the invoice to recur (e.g., daily, weekly, monthly), the start date, end date (if applicable), and any other recurrence details.
  - Review and Save: Double-check all the details to ensure accuracy, then click the "Save template" or "Save and close" button to save your recurring invoice.
  - Activate Recurring Invoice: After saving the template, you'll typically have the option to activate it immediately or leave it inactive. If you're ready for the recurring invoice to start generating invoices, activate it.
  - Monitor Recurring Invoices: Once activated, QuickBooks Online will automatically generate and send invoices at the intervals you've set. You can monitor and manage these recurring invoices from the Recurring Transactions section under the Sales tab.

- **Use Batch Invoicing:**
  - Navigate to Customers Tab: Log in to your QuickBooks Online account and click on the "Sales" tab in the left-hand navigation menu.
  - Select Customers: Within the Sales tab, click on "Customers."
  - Choose Batch Actions: On the Customers page, find and click on the "Batch actions" dropdown menu.
  - Select Create Batch Invoices: From the dropdown menu, select "Create batch invoices."
  - Select Customers: Choose the customers you want to invoice in batch. You can select multiple customers by checking the boxes next to their names.
  - Add Items/Services: For each selected customer, add the items or services you want to invoice them for. You can choose from your existing products and services list.
  - Review and Customize: Review the invoices to ensure accuracy. You can customize each invoice if needed, such as adding personalized messages or adjusting quantities.
  - Send Invoices: Once you're satisfied with the invoices, you can choose to save them as drafts, print them, or send them directly to the customers via email.
  - Review and Monitor: After sending the batch invoices, you can monitor their status and track payments in the "Invoices" section under the Sales tab.

Step 4: Streamline Invoice Management

- **Auto-Fill Customer Details:**
  - o Ensure that customer details are complete and up-to-date in the "Customer Center."
  - o When creating an invoice, start typing a customer's name and select them from the dropdown to autofill their details.
- **Set Product/Service Defaults:**
  - o Navigate to Products and Services: Log in to your QuickBooks Online account and click on the "Sales" tab in the left-hand navigation menu. Then select "Products and Services."
  - o Select Product/Service: Find the product or service for which you want to set defaults and click on it to open its details.

- o Edit Defaults: Once you're on the product or service details page, click on the "Edit" button.
- o Set Default Details: In the edit mode, you'll see various fields such as description, sales price/rate, income account, etc. Set these fields to the values you want as defaults for this product/service.
- o Save Changes: After updating the default details, make sure to click the "Save" button to save your changes.

Step 5: Manage Invoice Delivery and Tracking

- **Email Invoices Directly:**
  - When creating an invoice, check the "Email Later" box if you're batching or click "Email" to send it immediately.
  - Customize the email template under "Edit" > "Preferences" > "Send Forms" to include a payment link.
- **Track Email Status:**
  - Use the "Sent Email" feature in QuickBooks to monitor when invoices are sent and viewed by the customer.
- **Attach Necessary Documents:**
  - When creating or editing an invoice, use the "Attach File" button to add additional documents like contracts or receipts.

Step 6: Follow Up and Manage Payments

- **Automate Payment Reminders:**
  - In the "Customers" menu, select "Customer Center" and choose "Set Payment Reminders."
  - Create schedules and reminder messages that will automatically be sent to your customers before the due date.
- **Customize Late Fees:**
  - Under "Edit" > "Preferences" > "Finance Charge," set up rules for applying late fees to overdue invoices, specifying the amount and the conditions under which they apply.

Step 7: Enable Client Self-Service

- **Use the QuickBooks Online Portal:**
  - Enable the portal feature from "Edit" > "Preferences" > "Sales & Customers."
  - Invite customers to the portal by sending them an email invitation through QuickBooks, which allows them to view, download, and pay their invoices.

Step 8: Monitor and Report

- **Track Payment Status:**
  - o Use the "Income Tracker" in QuickBooks to view outstanding and paid invoices.
- **Run Aging Reports:**
  - o Go to "Reports" > "Customers & Receivables" > "A/R Aging Summary" to view overdue invoices and assess the financial health of your receivables.

Step 9: Integrate and Sync

- **Sync with Other Software:**
  - o Use the "Apps" menu to find and integrate compatible software like Xero, FreshBooks, or CRM systems that can enhance your QuickBooks setup.
- **Explore Automation Tools:**
  - o Connect apps like Zapier to automate workflows between QuickBooks and other services like email platforms or customer support tools.

Step 10: Ensure Accuracy and Security

- **Regularly Reconcile Transactions:**
  - o Regularly compare QuickBooks records with your bank statements to ensure all transactions are accurately recorded.
- **Maintain Data Security:**
  - o Use secure payment processing options and regularly update user permissions and access controls to protect sensitive information.

Generating Sales Receipts

Generating sales receipts in QuickBooks is a straightforward process that allows you to record sales transactions when customers pay in full at the time of purchase. Here's a step-by-step guide on how to generate sales receipts:

Log into QuickBooks Online

- Open your web browser and go to the QuickBooks Online login page.
- Enter your username and password to access your account.

Navigate to the Sales Receipts Page

- Once logged in, go to the QuickBooks Online dashboard.
- Click on the "+" icon or the "New" button to create a new transaction.

Select "Sales Receipt"

- In the "Customers" section, click on "Sales Receipt" from the dropdown menu.
- This will open a new sales receipt form for you to fill out.

Fill Out the Sales Receipt Form

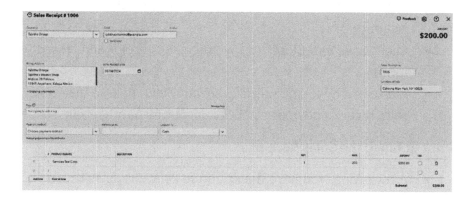

- **Customer Information:** Select the customer from the "Customer" dropdown menu or add a new customer if necessary.
- **Sales Receipt Date:** Enter the date of the sale. This is usually the date when the customer made the purchase.
- **Payment Method:** Choose the payment method from the dropdown menu (e.g., Cash, Check, Credit Card).
- **Product/Service:** Add the products or services sold by clicking on the "Product/Service" column. You can select items from your inventory list or add new ones on the spot.
- **Quantity:** Enter the quantity of each item sold.
- **Rate:** Input the selling price or rate for each item.
- **Description:** Optionally, add a description for each item to provide more details to the customer.
- **Tax:** If applicable, select the tax rate for the items sold.
- **Total:** QuickBooks will automatically calculate the total amount based on the quantity and rate.
- **Payment Details:** If the customer paid partially, you can enter the partial payment amount and the remaining balance.

Review and Save

- Double-check all the information on the sales receipt for accuracy.
- Click "Save and Close" to save the sales receipt and close the form.
- Alternatively, you can click "Save and New" to save the current sales receipt and open a new, blank one for another transaction.

Print or Email the Sales Receipt

- After saving, you have the option to print the sales receipt for your records or to give it to the customer.
- You can also email the sales receipt directly to the customer by clicking on the "Save and Send" button.

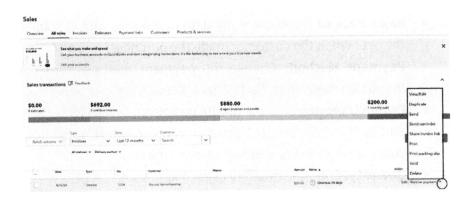

View and Manage Sales Receipts

- To view all your sales receipts, go to the "Sales" or "Customers" tab in QuickBooks Online.
- You can filter and search for specific sales receipts by customer, date, or transaction type.
- Edit or void sales receipts if there are any errors or if a refund is issued.

Tips for Generating Sales Receipts Efficiently

- **Use Default Settings:** Set default customer details, payment methods, and tax rates to speed up the process.
- **Recurring Sales Receipts:** For regular customers or subscriptions, set up recurring sales receipts to automate the process.
- **Mobile App:** QuickBooks Online mobile app allows you to create sales receipts on-the-go, perfect for retail businesses or events.
- **Integration with Payment Processors:** Link QuickBooks to your payment processor to automatically record sales receipts when payments are received online.

Managing Customer Payments

Managing customer payments in QuickBooks is essential for keeping track of incoming revenue, reconciling accounts, and maintaining accurate financial records. Here's a detailed guide on how to manage customer payments effectively:

Log into QuickBooks Online:

- Open your web browser and log into your QuickBooks Online account using your credentials.

Navigate to the "Sales" Menu:

- From the QuickBooks Online dashboard, locate and click on the "All Sales" or "Invoicing" tab in the left-hand menu.

View Outstanding Invoices:

- Click on "Invoices" to view a list of all your outstanding invoices awaiting payment. Review the list to see which invoices are due for payment from customers.

Record Customer Payments:

- To record a customer payment, click on the "Receive Payment" button or the "+" icon. Select the customer from the "Customer" dropdown menu for whom you are recording the payment.

Enter Payment Details: Payment Date: Enter the date when the payment was received.

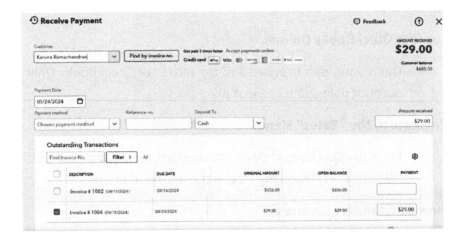

- **Payment Method:** Choose the payment method from the dropdown menu (e.g., Cash, Check, Credit Card).
- **Reference Number:** Optionally, enter a reference number for the payment (e.g., check number, transaction ID).

- **Amount Received:** Input the amount that the customer paid.
- **Apply to Invoices:** Check the box next to the invoices you want to apply the payment to.
- **Discounts or Credits:** If applicable, you can apply discounts or credits to the payment.

Review and Save

- Double-check all the payment details to ensure accuracy.
- Click "Save and Close" to save the customer payment and close the window.
- Alternatively, click "Save and New" to save the payment and open a new payment form.

View Payment Transactions

- To view all recorded customer payments, go to the "Sales" or "Customers" tab.
- Click on "Customers" to see a list of customers and their payment statuses.
- You can also view individual customer profiles to see their payment history.

Apply Payments to Specific Invoices

- QuickBooks automatically matches payments to open invoices based on the customer name and amount.
- You can manually select which invoices to apply the payment to by unchecking or checking the boxes next to each invoice.

Partial Payments and Overpayments

- QuickBooks allows you to record partial payments for invoices.
- If a customer pays less than the full invoice amount, enter the partial payment amount.
- For overpayments, QuickBooks will show a credit on the customer's account, which can be applied to future invoices.

Print or Email Payment Receipts

- After saving the customer payment, you have the option to print a receipt for the customer.
- Click on the "Print" icon to generate a payment receipt that you can give to the customer.
- Alternatively, you can email the payment receipt directly to the customer by clicking on the "Email" option.

Reconcile Bank Accounts

- To ensure accuracy, regularly reconcile your bank accounts with your recorded transactions.
- Go to the "Transactions" > "BankTransactions" and select "Reconcile" to match bank transactions with QuickBooks entries or go to "Transactions" and select "Reconcile" (depending on your version).

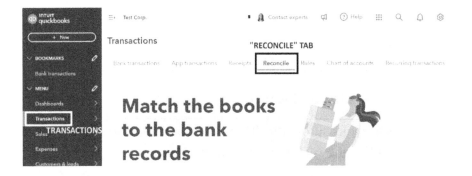

Apply Discounts or Write-Offs

- If you offer discounts for early payments or need to write off uncollectible invoices, you can do so within the payment window.
- Click on "Discounts and Credits" to apply discounts, credits, or write-offs to the payment.

Manage Undeposited Funds

- When recording customer payments, QuickBooks often places the funds in the "Undeposited Funds" account.
- To deposit these funds into your bank account, go to the "Banking" or "Accounting" tab and select "Make Deposits."

Recurring Payments and Auto-Application

- For regular customers with recurring payments, set up recurring customer payments to automate the process.
- QuickBooks can also automatically apply payments to invoices based on the rules you set up.

Customer Payment Reports

- Generate reports to track customer payments, outstanding balances, and payment trends.
- Go to the "Reports" tab and select "Sales" or "Customers" reports to view payment history and aging summaries.

Reversing or Deleting Payments

- If you need to reverse or delete a recorded customer payment, locate the payment transaction and click on "More" or "Delete."
- Note that deleted transactions cannot be recovered, so exercise caution.

Tips for Efficient Customer Payment Management

- **Regular Updates:** Keep customer payment records up to date to ensure accurate financial reporting.
- **Automated Reminders:** Set up payment reminders for overdue invoices to encourage timely payments.
- **Batch Payments:** If you receive multiple payments from the same customer, consider batching them for efficiency.

- **Integrated Payment Processors:** Integrate QuickBooks with payment processors for seamless recording of online payments.
- **Customer Communication:** Clearly communicate payment terms, due dates, and accepted payment methods to customers.

Automating Recurring Sales Documents

Automating recurring sales documents, such as invoices or sales receipts, in QuickBooks can save you time and effort by automatically generating and sending these documents to customers on a regular schedule. Here's a step-by-step guide on how to set up recurring sales documents in QuickBooks Online:

Log into QuickBooks Online

- Open your web browser and log into your QuickBooks Online account using your credentials.

Navigate to the "Sales" Menu

- From the QuickBooks Online dashboard, locate and click on the "Sales" or "Transactions" tab in the left-hand menu.

Create a New Recurring Sales Document

- **Navigate to the Sales Tab**: Log in to your QuickBooks Online account and click on the "Sales" or "Transactions" tab in the left-hand navigation menu.
- **Select Recurring Transactions**: Within the Transaction (or Sales) tab, you'll see several options. Look for and click on "Recurring Transactions."
- **Click New Recurring Transaction**: Once you're in the Recurring Transactions section, you'll see a list of any existing recurring transactions. To create a new one, click on the "New Recurring Transaction" or "New" button, usually located at the top-right corner of the page.

- **Choose Document Type**: QuickBooks Online offers several types of recurring sales documents, such as invoices, sales receipts, or estimates. Select the type of document you want to create from the dropdown menu.

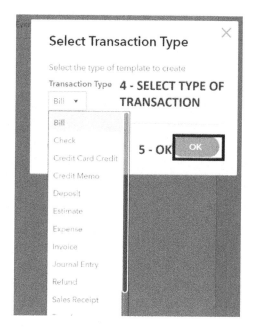

- **Fill in Transaction Details**: Now, you'll need to fill in the details of your recurring sales document. This includes information such as customer name, products or services sold, quantities, prices, and any other relevant details.
- **Set Recurrence Schedule**: Below the transaction details, you'll find options to set the recurrence schedule for the document. Choose how often you want the document to recur (e.g., daily, weekly, monthly) and specify the start date, end date (if applicable), and any other recurrence details.

- **Review and Save**: Once you've entered all the necessary information and set the recurrence schedule, review everything to ensure accuracy. Then, click the "Save template" or "Save and close" button to save your recurring sales document.
- **Activate Recurring Transaction**: After saving the template, you'll typically have the option to activate it immediately or leave it inactive. If you're ready for the recurring sales document to start generating transactions, activate it.
- **Monitor Recurring Transactions**: Once activated, QuickBooks Online will automatically generate the specified sales document at the intervals you've set. You can monitor and manage these recurring transactions from the Recurring Transactions section under the Sales tab.

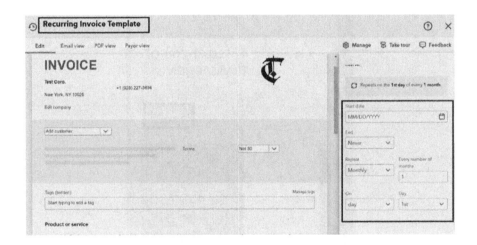

Set Up Recurring Sales Document Details

- **Customer Information:** Choose the customer for whom you want to create the recurring sales document.
- **Template Customization:** Customize the template by adding your logo, company information, and personalized messages.
- **Products/Services:** Add the products or services you want to include in the recurring document.
- **Frequency:** Select the frequency of the recurring document (e.g., Weekly, Monthly, Quarterly).

- **Start Date:** Specify the start date for the recurring document schedule.
- **End Date:** Optionally, set an end date for the recurring document schedule. Leave blank for ongoing recurrence.

Specify Document Delivery Method

- **Email:** Choose to email the recurring sales document directly to the customer.
- **Print and Mail:** Select this option if you want to print and mail the document to the customer yourself.

Review and Save the Recurring Sales Document

- Double-check all the details of the recurring sales document for accuracy.
- Click "Save and Close" to save the recurring document and close the window.
- Alternatively, click "Save and New" to save the current document and create another recurring document.

View and Manage Recurring Sales Documents

- To view all your recurring sales documents, go to the "Sales" or "Customers" tab.
- Click on "Recurring Transactions" or "Scheduled Transactions" to see a list of all scheduled documents.
- From here, you can edit, pause, or delete recurring documents as needed.

Edit or Modify Recurring Sales Documents

- To make changes to a recurring sales document, locate it in the list of recurring transactions.
- Click on the document to open it, then make the necessary edits to customer information, items, frequency, or delivery method.
- Save the changes to update the recurring document.

Pause or Stop Recurring Sales Documents

- If you need to temporarily pause a recurring sales document, locate it in the list of recurring transactions.
- Click on the document to open it, then select the "Pause" option.
- To stop a recurring document entirely, select the "Delete" or "End" option and confirm.

Customer Communication and Notifications

- Notify customers about the recurring sales documents and their schedules.
- Send reminders or notifications about upcoming payments or deliveries.

Tips for Efficient Recurring Sales Document Management

- **Regular Review:** Periodically review and update recurring sales documents to ensure accuracy and relevance.
- **Bulk Edit:** Use QuickBooks' bulk editing tools to make changes to multiple recurring documents at once.
- **Automated Payment Integration:** Link recurring invoices with payment processors for automatic billing and payment collection.
- **Customer Preferences:** Consider customer preferences for document delivery (email, mail) and customize accordingly.
- **Communication:** Clearly communicate recurring document details, payment terms, and delivery schedules with customers.

Recording Sales Transactions

Recording sales transactions in QuickBooks Online is crucial for tracking income, managing accounts receivable, and maintaining accurate financial records. Here's a step-by-step guide on how to record sales transactions, such as invoices and sales receipts, in QuickBooks Online:

Log into QuickBooks Online

- Open your web browser and log into your QuickBooks Online account using your credentials.

Navigate to the "Sales" Menu

- From the QuickBooks Online dashboard, locate and click on the "Sales" or "Invoicing" tab in the left-hand menu.

Create a New Sales Transaction

Create an Invoice:

- Click on the "+" icon or the "New Transaction" button to create a new transaction.
- Select "Invoice" from the dropdown menu under "New Transaction" button.

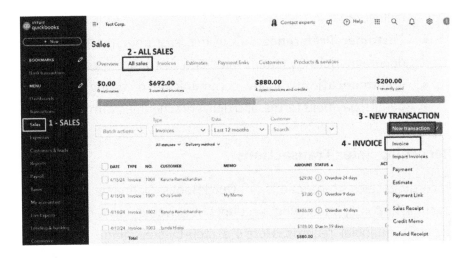

Create a Sales Receipt:

- Alternatively, if the customer pays in full at the time of purchase, select "Sales Receipt" instead of "Invoice."

Enter Customer Information

- In the "Customer" field, select the customer for whom you are creating the sales transaction.
- If the customer is new, you can add their details by clicking on the "+ Add New" option.

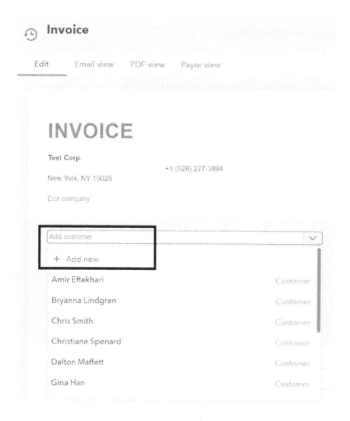

Add Products or Services Sold

- In the "Product/Service" column, select the item(s) that the customer purchased.
- If the item is not on the list, you can add a new product or service on the spot.

Enter Quantity and Rate

- For each product or service, enter the quantity sold and the unit price or rate.
- QuickBooks will automatically calculate the total amount for each line item.

Add Descriptions (Optional)

- Optionally, you can add descriptions for each line item to provide more details to the customer.

Specify Tax Rate (If Applicable)

- If the items are taxable, select the appropriate tax rate from the "Tax" dropdown menu.
- QuickBooks will calculate the tax amount based on the taxable items.

Review and Save the Sales Transaction

- Double-check all the details of the sales transaction for accuracy.
- Click "Save and Close" to save the transaction and close the window.
- Alternatively, click "Save and New" to save the current transaction and open a new one.

Print or Email the Sales Document

- After saving the sales transaction, you have the option to print the document for your records or to give it to the customer.
- You can also email the sales document directly to the customer by clicking on the "Save and Send" button.

View and Manage Sales Transactions

- To view all your recorded sales transactions, go to the "Sales" or "Customers" tab.
- Click on "Invoices" or "Sales Receipts" to see a list of all transactions.
- From here, you can filter, search, and manage individual sales transactions.

Apply Payments to Invoices (For Invoices)

If you've created an invoice, customers can pay later. Once they do:

- Go to the "Sales" or "Customers" tab and select "Receive Payment."
- Choose the customer, select the invoice, enter the payment amount, and save the transaction.

Track Payments and Receivables

- Monitor the status of payments and outstanding balances in the "Customers" tab.
- Run reports such as "Aging Receivables" to track overdue payments and outstanding invoices.

Tips for Efficient Sales Transaction Recording:

- Use Default Settings: Set default customer details, tax rates, and invoice templates for quicker transactions.
- Bulk Add Products: If you have multiple line items, use the "Copy" or "Duplicate" feature to save time.
- Recurring Transactions: For subscription-based services or regular billing, set up recurring invoices to automate the process.
- Integrated Payment Processing: Link QuickBooks with payment processors for easy and automatic recording of online payments.
- Customer Communication: Clearly communicate invoice details, payment terms, and due dates with customers.

Troubleshooting Common Issues

Troubleshooting common issues in QuickBooks can help resolve many problems that users encounter. Here are some of the most common issues and their potential solutions:

QuickBooks Running Slowly:

- Check your system requirements. QuickBooks might be slow if your computer doesn't meet the minimum requirements.
- Clean up your company file. Large or cluttered files can slow down QuickBooks. You can condense the file to remove old transactions.
- Check for updates. Make sure you are using the latest version of QuickBooks, as updates often include performance improvements.
- Turn off unnecessary features. Disable features you don't use to reduce the load on the software.

QuickBooks Company File Issues:

For QuickBooks Online, managing company file issues is a bit different than the desktop version. Here's what you can do:

1. **Run the Reconciliation Discrepancy Tool**: This tool helps identify and fix issues with reconciled transactions. Go to the "Accounting" menu, then "Reconcile." Select "History by account" and then "Reconciliation Report" for the account with issues. Click on "Reconciliation Discrepancy" to run the tool.
2. **Review Audit Log**: The Audit Log tracks changes made to your company file. Reviewing it can help identify and rectify any unintended changes or errors. Go to the "Settings" menu, then "Audit Log" to access this feature.
3. **Contact QuickBooks Support**: If you encounter persistent or complex issues with your QuickBooks Online company file, reaching out to QuickBooks Support can provide tailored

assistance. They can offer guidance specific to your situation and help resolve the issue effectively.

Remember, regular backups of your QuickBooks Online data are essential to safeguard against data loss. If all else fails, restoring from a recent backup can often resolve many issues.

QuickBooks Error Codes

- Look up the error code. QuickBooks has a vast database of error codes with explanations and potential solutions. Search for the error code on the Intuit support website or community forums.
- Update QuickBooks. Many error codes are fixed in newer versions of the software.
- Contact QuickBooks Support. If you can't resolve the issue on your own, Intuit's support team can often provide assistance.

QuickBooks Connection Issues

- Check your internet connection. Ensure you have a stable and active internet connection.
- Update QuickBooks to the latest version. New updates often include fixes for connectivity issues.
- Reset your network settings. Sometimes, resetting your router or modem can resolve connectivity problems.

QuickBooks Reconciliation Problems

- Check for discrepancies. Review your transactions and make sure they match your bank statements.
- Undo the last reconciliation. If you've reconciled incorrectly, you can undo the reconciliation and start over.
- Go to the Banking menu, then Reconcile.
- Click on the appropriate account, then click "Undo Last Reconciliation."

CHAPTER 4
EXPENSES AND VENDORS

Recording and Categorizing Expenses

Introduction to Expense Management in QBO

Expense management in QuickBooks Online (QBO) is a crucial aspect of maintaining accurate financial records for your business. It involves tracking, categorizing, and managing the expenses incurred by your business operations. Here's an introduction to expense management in QBO:

Recording Expenses:

- To record an expense in QBO, you'll typically start by clicking on the "New" button and then selecting "Expense" under the "Vendors" or "+ New" menu.

- Enter the necessary details, such as the payee, date of the expense, payment method, and the account to which the expense should be attributed.
- You can also attach receipts or documents to the expense entry for record-keeping purposes.

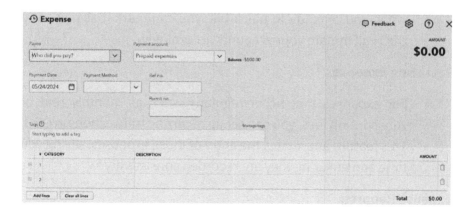

Categorizing Expenses:

- Properly categorizing expenses helps you track where your money is going and analyze spending patterns.
- QBO provides predefined expense categories, but you can also create custom categories that suit your business needs.
- Common expense categories include office supplies, rent, utilities, travel, meals, and advertising.

Bank Feeds for Expense Tracking:

- QBO allows you to connect your bank and credit card accounts, enabling automatic import of transactions.
- When expenses appear in your bank feeds, you can review and match them to existing records or create new expense entries.
- This feature streamlines the process of tracking expenses and ensures accuracy in your financial records.

Bill Management:

- If you receive bills from vendors that you need to pay later, you can enter them in QBO using the "Bill" feature.
- QBO will keep track of your upcoming bills, their due dates, and the total amounts owed.
- When you're ready to pay a bill, you can mark it as paid, and QBO will update your accounts accordingly.

Recurring Expenses:

- For expenses that occur regularly, such as monthly rent or subscription fees, you can set up recurring transactions in QBO.
- This feature automates the entry of these expenses, saving you time and ensuring they are recorded consistently.

Expense Reports:

- QBO allows you to generate detailed expense reports, which provide insights into your business's spending habits.

- You can customize these reports to show specific time periods, expense categories, or payees.
- Expense reports are useful for budgeting, tax preparation, and analyzing cost-saving opportunities.

Integration with Receipt Capture Apps:

- QBO integrates with various receipt capture apps such as Receipt Bank, Expensify, and Hubdoc.
- These apps allow you to snap pictures of receipts with your smartphone, which are then automatically synced with QBO.
- This eliminates manual data entry and ensures that all expenses are accurately recorded.

Tax Deductions and Compliance:

- Properly managing expenses in QBO helps ensure that you can claim legitimate tax deductions.
- QBO also helps you stay compliant with tax regulations by organizing expenses in a way that makes it easier to prepare tax returns.

Audit Trails and Security:

- QBO maintains a detailed audit trail of all expense transactions, showing who entered, modified, or deleted them.
- This ensures accountability and helps prevent fraud or errors.
- QBO also employs robust security measures to protect your financial data.

Training and Support:

- QuickBooks Online offers a range of resources, tutorials, and webinars to help you learn more about expense management.
- If you encounter any issues or have questions, you can reach out to QuickBooks support for assistance.

Setting Up Expense Accounts

Setting up expense accounts in QuickBooks is an essential part of organizing your business's finances. Expense accounts help you categorize and track the money spent on various business activities, such as supplies, utilities, rent, travel, and more. Here's how you can set up expense accounts in QuickBooks:

Access Chart of Accounts:

- Log in to your QuickBooks Online account.
- Navigate to the "Transaction" → "Chart of Accounts" section. This can typically be found in the left-hand menu.

Add a New Expense Account:

- Once you're in the Chart of Accounts, look for the "New" button. Click on it to create a new account.

- Select "Expense" as the account type. This type is used for tracking money spent on business-related expenses.
- You'll then be prompted to enter details for the new expense account.

Enter Account Details:

- **Account Name:** Enter a name for the expense account. This should clearly identify the type of expense it represents, such as "Utilities," "Rent," "Repairs & Maintenance," etc.
- **Account Type:** Choose "Expense" from the drop-down menu.
- **Detail Type:** This is a more specific categorization of the account. QuickBooks provides a list of detail types to choose from, such as "Advertising," "Office Supplies," "Travel," etc.
- **Description (Optional):** You can add a description to provide more details about the account if needed.

Save the New Expense Account:

- Once you've entered all the necessary details, click on "Save and Close" or "Save and New" to save the new expense account.
- QuickBooks will now add the new expense account to your Chart of Accounts.

Repeat for Additional Expense Accounts:

- If you have more expense categories to create, repeat the process for each one.
- This allows you to set up a comprehensive list of expense accounts tailored to your business's needs.

Editing or Deleting Expense Accounts:

- If you need to edit an expense account, you can go back to the Chart of Accounts, find the account, and select "Edit."
- To delete an expense account, choose "Delete" from the drop-down menu next to the account. Note that you can only delete an account if it has no transactions associated with it.

Example of Expense Accounts:

Here are examples of common expense accounts you might set up:

- Advertising
- Office Supplies
- Rent
- Utilities
- Travel
- Meals & Entertainment
- Repairs & Maintenance
- Insurance
- Professional Fees

Tips for Organizing Expense Accounts:

- **Be Specific:** Create expense accounts that are specific to the types of expenses your business incurs. This makes it easier to track and analyze spending.

- **Use Subaccounts:** If you have subcategories within an expense type, consider creating subaccounts. For example, "Travel" could have subaccounts for "Airfare," "Lodging," "Meals," etc.
- **Maintain Consistency:** Use consistent naming conventions for your expense accounts to avoid confusion and ensure clarity in your financial reports.
- **Review Regularly:** Periodically review your expense accounts to ensure they still reflect your business's needs. You can edit, merge, or deactivate accounts as needed.

Recording Expenses

Recording expenses in QuickBooks Online (QBO) is a fundamental task for keeping accurate financial records. Here's a step-by-step guide on how to record expenses:

Navigate to the Expenses Tab:

- Log in to your QuickBooks Online account.
- From the left-hand menu, select "Expenses" and then "Expenses."

Click on "New Expense":

- On the Expenses page, click on the "New Transaction" button, usually located in the upper-right corner.

Enter Expense Details:

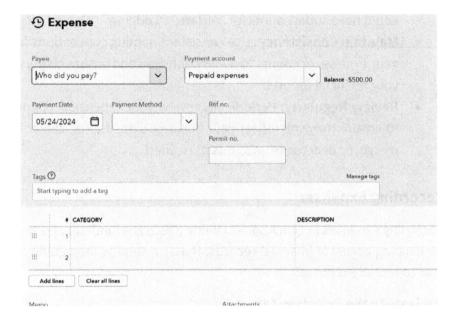

- **Payee:** Choose the name of the vendor or supplier from the drop-down list. If it's a new vendor, you can add them by selecting "Add new" or "Add manually."
- **Payment Date:** Enter the date the expense was incurred or the date of the payment.
- **Payment Method:** Select the method of payment, such as credit card, cash, check, or bank transfer.
- **Category:** Choose the appropriate expense category from the drop-down list. This is where you'll select one of the expense accounts you previously set up (e.g., "Office Supplies," "Utilities," "Rent," etc.).
- **Amount:** Enter the total amount of the expense.
- **Tax Deductible:** If the expense is tax-deductible, you can mark it as such.
- **Description (Optional):** Add a description of the expense, including any relevant details.

Attach Receipt (Optional):

- You can attach a digital copy of the receipt or invoice for the expense.
- Click on the "Attach Receipt" button, then upload the file from your computer or cloud storage.

Save the Expense:

- Once you've entered all the details, click on the "Save" button to record the expense.

Expense Reports:

- After recording expenses, you can generate detailed expense reports in QuickBooks Online.
- Go to the "Reports" tab, then select "Standard," and choose "Expenses by Vendor Summary" or "Expenses by Account."
- Customize the report by date range, vendors, expense accounts, and more.

Mobile App:

- If you're on the go, you can use the QuickBooks Online mobile app to record expenses.
- Simply open the app, select "Expenses," and follow similar steps to enter the expense details.
- You can also capture and attach photos of receipts directly from your phone.

Reconciling Accounts:

- Regularly reconcile your bank and credit card accounts in QuickBooks Online to ensure that all expenses are accurately recorded.
- This process helps identify any discrepancies between your records and bank statements.

Additional Tips:

- Splitting Expenses: If an expense needs to be split between multiple categories or accounts, you can select "Split" and allocate the amounts accordingly.
- Recurring Expenses: For expenses that occur regularly, such as monthly rent or subscription fees, you can set them up as recurring transactions.
- Mileage Tracking: QuickBooks Online also allows you to track and record mileage expenses for business trips. You can find this feature under the "Mileage" tab within Expenses.
- Bank Feeds: If you've connected your bank account to QuickBooks Online, you can match the recorded expense with the corresponding transaction in your bank feeds. This helps keep your accounts in sync.

Categorizing Expenses

Categorizing expenses in QuickBooks Online (QBO) is a crucial step in organizing your business finances. Proper categorization helps you track where your money is going, analyze spending patterns, and prepare accurate financial reports. Here's how you can categorize expenses in QBO:

Recording an Expense:

- Start by navigating to the "Expenses" or "Transactions" tab in QBO.
- Click on "New Transaction" or "New Expense" to create a new expense entry (see previous picture)

Choose Expense Account:

- In the expense form, you'll see a field labeled "Category." This is where you select the appropriate expense account for the transaction.

- Click on the drop-down menu under "Category" to view a list of your expense accounts.

Select the Correct Expense Account:

- Choose the account that best fits the nature of the expense. This could include categories like "Office Supplies," "Travel," "Advertising," "Utilities," "Rent," and more.
- If you don't see the exact category you need, you can create a new one by clicking on "Add new" or "Add manually" in the drop-down menu.

Use Subcategories (Optional):

- If you have more specific types of expenses within a category, you can use subcategories.
- For example, under "Travel," you might have subcategories like "Airfare," "Lodging," "Meals," etc.
- To create a subcategory, select "Add new" when choosing a category and mark it as a subcategory.

Save the Expense:

- Once you've selected the appropriate expense account, enter the amount, date, payee/vendor, payment method, and any other relevant details.
- Click "Save" or "Save and Close" to record the expense with the chosen category.

Subcategorizing Expenses:

- To create a subcategory, select "Add new" when choosing a category for an expense.
- Check the box that says "Is subcategory" to indicate that it's a subcategory of another expense account.
- You can nest subcategories under main categories to create a hierarchical structure.

Reviewing Categorized Expenses:

- After recording expenses, you can run expense reports in QBO to review categorized transactions.
- Go to the "Reports" tab, select "Standard," and choose reports such as "Expenses by Vendor Summary" or "Expenses by Account."
- Customize the reports by date range, vendors, accounts, and more to get the desired insights.

Tips for Categorizing Expenses:

- **Be Specific:** Use specific categories that accurately describe the nature of the expense. This helps with tracking and analysis.
- **Consistency:** Maintain consistent naming conventions for your expense accounts. This ensures clarity and avoids confusion when reviewing reports.
- **Review Regularly:** Periodically review your expense categories to make sure they still align with your business needs. You can edit or add new categories as your business evolves.
- **Customize Categories:** Customize the list of expense accounts to match your business's unique expenses. QBO allows you to create, edit, and delete accounts as needed.

- **Group Similar Expenses:** Group similar expenses together under a broader category. For example, "Utilities" might include electricity, water, and gas bills.

Benefits of Proper Categorization:

- **Accurate Financial Reports:** Categorized expenses ensure that your financial reports reflect the true financial status of your business.
- **Tax Compliance:** Properly categorized expenses make it easier to identify tax-deductible expenses, ensuring you're compliant with tax regulations.
- **Budgeting and Forecasting:** Categorized expenses provide valuable data for budgeting purposes and forecasting future expenses.
- **Analysis and Decision-Making:** Analyzing categorized expenses helps you make informed decisions about cost-cutting, investments, and business strategies.

CHAPTER 5
PAYROLL AND EMPLOYEES

Setting Up Payroll in QuickBooks Online

Introduction to Payroll in QBO and Setup Process

Payroll in QuickBooks Online (QBO) streamlines the process of paying your employees, calculating taxes, and keeping track of payroll-related expenses. It's an essential feature for businesses of all sizes. Here's an introduction to payroll in QBO and the setup process:

Overview of Payroll in QBO:

- QuickBooks Online offers a comprehensive payroll system that allows you to manage employee salaries, deductions, taxes, and compliance with ease.
- You can run payroll, generate paychecks or direct deposits, file payroll taxes, and keep accurate records—all within the same platform.

Setting Up Payroll:

Verify Payroll Subscription:

- Ensure you have an active payroll subscription with QuickBooks Online. If not, you'll need to subscribe to a payroll plan.

Access Payroll Setup:

- Log in to your QuickBooks Online account.
- Navigate to the "Employees" or "Payroll" tab in the left-hand menu.

Start Payroll Setup:

- Click on "Employees" or "Payroll Setup," depending on your version of QuickBooks Online.
- Follow the guided setup process to enter essential information about your company, employees, and tax details.

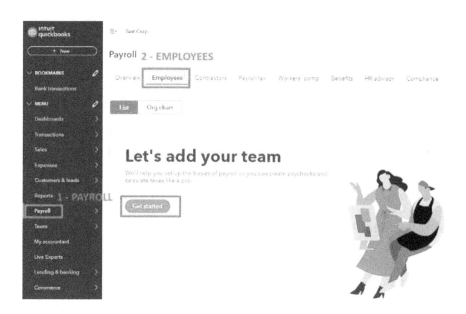

Enter Company Information:

- Provide basic information about your business, including legal name, business address, Federal Employer Identification Number (FEIN), and state tax ID numbers.

Add Employees:

- Enter details for each employee, such as name, address, Social Security Number (SSN), pay rate, pay schedule (weekly, bi-weekly, monthly), and any deductions or contributions.
- You can also set up direct deposit for employees if desired.

Tax Setup:

- QuickBooks Online automatically calculates federal and state payroll taxes based on the information you provide.
- Enter tax details such as filing status, allowances, and additional withholding amounts for each employee.
- Verify state and local tax rates and requirements for accurate calculations.

Benefits and Deductions:

- Set up employee benefits such as health insurance, retirement plans, and other deductions like garnishments or union dues.
- Enter the contribution amounts or percentages, and QuickBooks will deduct these amounts from employee paychecks.

Payroll Schedule:

- Choose your preferred payroll schedule, whether it's weekly, bi-weekly, semi-monthly, or monthly.
- This schedule determines how often you'll run payroll and when employees will receive their pay.

Payment Methods:

- Decide how you want to pay your employees—via direct deposit or printed checks.
- Set up bank account information for direct deposit payments.

Running Payroll:

Enter Employee Hours:

- Before running payroll, enter the hours worked by each employee for the pay period.
- You can also use timesheets, if enabled, to track employee hours.

Review and Approve:

- Preview the payroll summary to ensure accuracy.
- Verify employee hours, wages, deductions, and taxes.
- Make any necessary adjustments before finalizing payroll.

Process Payroll:

- Once everything looks correct, click "Run Payroll" to process employee paychecks.
- QuickBooks Online will calculate net pay, deductions, and taxes automatically.

Pay Employees:

- After processing payroll, you can choose to pay employees via direct deposit or print checks.
- QuickBooks will generate pay stubs for employees detailing their earnings and deductions.

Payroll Taxes and Forms:

Tax Filings:

- QuickBooks Online calculates and withholds federal, state, and local payroll taxes for you.
- The system also provides reminders and deadlines for tax payments.

Tax Forms:

- QBO generates and files payroll tax forms such as W-2s, 1099s, 941s, and state tax forms.
- You can e-file these forms directly from QuickBooks Online for added convenience.

Compliance:

- Stay compliant with federal and state labor laws and regulations.
- QuickBooks Online updates tax tables and rates automatically to reflect changes in tax laws.

Reports and Insights:

Payroll Reports:

- QBO offers a variety of payroll reports, including payroll summaries, tax liability reports, and employee earnings reports.
- These reports provide insights into your labor costs, tax obligations, and employee compensation.

Budgeting and Forecasting:

- Use payroll data to create budgets, forecast expenses, and plan for future growth.
- Analyze trends in employee costs and adjust your financial strategy accordingly.

Support and Resources:

Help Center:

- QuickBooks Online provides a Help Center with articles, guides, and tutorials on payroll setup and management.
- Access the Help Center for step-by-step instructions and troubleshooting tips.

Customer Support:

- If you encounter any issues or have questions, QuickBooks Online offers customer support via phone, chat, or email.
- Reach out to the support team for personalized assistance with your payroll setup.

Adding Employee Information

When you hire a new employee, there's a lot to handle—from paperwork to payroll. This guide simplifies how to add an employee to QuickBooks Online Payroll and QuickBooks Desktop Payroll, ensuring you cover all necessary steps from gathering information to entering it into the system.

Step 1: Gather Employee Information

Before adding an employee to your payroll, collect the following necessary documents and information:

- **W-4 Form**: Collect the Employee's Withholding Certificate for personal details like name, address, social security number, dependents, and adjustments. It's mandatory to keep a copy for your records.

Form W-4

Department of the Treasury
Internal Revenue Service

Employee's Withholding Certificate

Complete Form W-4 so that your employer can withhold the correct federal income tax from your pay.
Give Form W-4 to your employer.
Your withholding is subject to review by the IRS.

OMB No. 1545-0074

2024

Step 1: Enter Personal Information

(a) First name and middle initial | Last name

(b) Social security number

Address

Does your name match the name on your social security card? If not, to ensure you get credit for your earnings, contact SSA at 800-772-1213 or go to www.ssa.gov.

City or town, state, and ZIP code

(c)
☐ Single or Married filing separately
☐ Married filing jointly or Qualifying surviving spouse
☐ Head of household (Check only if you're unmarried and pay more than half the costs of keeping up a home for yourself and a qualifying individual.)

Complete Steps 2–4 ONLY if they apply to you; otherwise, skip to Step 5. See page 2 for more information on each step, who can claim exemption from withholding, and when to use the estimator at *www.irs.gov/W4App*.

Step 2: Multiple Jobs or Spouse Works

Complete this step if you (1) hold more than one job at a time, or (2) are married filing jointly and your spouse also works. The correct amount of withholding depends on income earned from all of these jobs.

Do **only one** of the following.

(a) Use the estimator at *www.irs.gov/W4App* for most accurate withholding for this step (and Steps 3–4). If you or your spouse have self-employment income, use this option; **or**

(b) Use the Multiple Jobs Worksheet on page 3 and enter the result in Step 4(c) below; **or**

(c) If there are only two jobs total, you may check this box. Do the same on Form W-4 for the other job. This option is generally more accurate than (b) if pay at the lower paying job is more than half of the pay at the higher paying job. Otherwise, (b) is more accurate . . . . ☐

Complete Steps 3–4(b) on Form W-4 for only ONE of these jobs. Leave those steps blank for the other jobs. (Your withholding will be most accurate if you complete Steps 3–4(b) on the Form W-4 for the highest paying job.)

- **I-9 Form**: Used to verify employment eligibility in the U.S. Ensure the employee has a valid Social Security number (not an ITIN).

- **Email Address**: Needed to invite the employee to add their personal information via QuickBooks and access their pay stubs and W-2s online.

- **Work Location**: Record the physical location where the employee will be working.

- **Pay Information**: Determine the employee's salary or wage rate, other compensation types, and the pay schedule.

- **Direct Deposit Information**: If applicable, collect the employee's bank routing and account numbers. Employees may add up to two bank accounts.

- **Pay History**: Required if this is your initial setup with QuickBooks payroll and you have already paid employees during the fiscal year.

Step 2: Add Your Employee in QuickBooks

QuickBooks Online Payroll:

- **Navigate to Payroll**: Go to the "Payroll" menu, then select "Employees" o click to "Employees" in the left-hand menu.
- **Add an Employee**: Click on "Add an Employee".

- **Enter Basic Info**: Input the employee's name and email address. Enable "Employee self-setup" if you prefer the employee to enter their personal, tax, and banking info. QuickBooks will send them an invite to join QuickBooks Workforce.

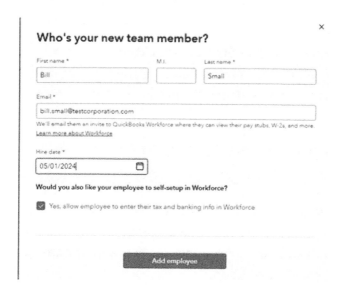

- **Complete the Setup**: Click on any section to add additional employee info. If "Employee self-setup" is enabled, certain fields may not be editable. You can turn off this feature in the "Personal Info" section to edit these fields.
- **Save**: Once all information is added, select "Save".

QuickBooks Desktop Payroll:

- **Set Employee Defaults** (Optional but Recommended):
  - o   Go to "Edit", then "Preferences".
  - o   Click on "Payroll and Employees", then "Company Preferences".
  - o   Select "Employee Defaults", make any necessary changes, and click "OK" twice to save.
- **Add Employee to Payroll:**
  - o   Open "Employees", then select "Employee Center".
  - o   Click on "New Employee" and enter all required information.
  - o   Press "OK" to save the employee profile.

Step 3: Complete New State Setup (if applicable)

If your new employee lives or works in a different state from where your business is located, you may need to setup and pay additional state taxes:

- **Follow any prompts from QuickBooks**: If you receive an email indicating new information is needed for company tax setup, follow the instructions provided to ensure compliance with state tax regulations.

Step 4: Invite Employees to Access Pay Stubs and W-2s

For employees to view and print their pay documents online:

- **Send an Invite via QuickBooks Workforce**: This can be set up during the employee addition process in QuickBooks Online or afterwards by navigating to the appropriate section and sending an invitation.

Tax Information and Compliance

Tax information and compliance are crucial aspects of managing your business finances, and QuickBooks Online (QBO) offers a range of features to help you stay organized, accurate, and compliant with tax regulations. Here's an overview of tax-related tools and steps to ensure compliance in QBO:

Tax Setup and Settings:

Company Tax Settings:

- Navigate to the "Taxes" or "Sales Tax" section in QuickBooks Online.

- Set up your company's tax settings, including tax agencies, filing frequencies, and tax ID numbers.

Sales Tax Setup:

- If your business collects sales tax, configure sales tax rates for each applicable jurisdiction.
- Specify the tax rates for different regions or products/services sold.

Tax Agencies:

- Add the tax agencies you're required to remit taxes to, such as federal, state, and local tax authorities.
- Ensure accurate details for each agency, including addresses, contact information, and tax ID numbers.

Sales Tax Tracking:

Automated Sales Tax:

- QuickBooks Online offers Automated Sales Tax for simplified sales tax management.
- The system calculates sales tax on sales transactions based on your configured rates and rules.

Sales Tax Reports:

- Generate sales tax reports to review collected sales tax by period, jurisdiction, or product/service.
- These reports help you reconcile your sales tax liabilities and prepare for tax filings.

Payroll Taxes:

Payroll Tax Setup:

- Set up your payroll tax settings, including federal, state, and local tax rates.
- Specify employee withholding allowances, deductions, and contributions.

Payroll Tax Forms:

- QBO generates and files payroll tax forms such as W-2s, 1099s, 941s, and state-specific forms.
- Review and e-file these forms directly from QuickBooks Online to meet filing deadlines.

Tax Payments:

- Schedule and make electronic payments for federal and state payroll taxes through QBO.
- Receive reminders for upcoming tax payments to avoid penalties and interest.

Income Tax Preparation:

Organize Financial Data:

- Categorize income, expenses, and deductions accurately throughout the year.
- Use the Chart of Accounts to maintain detailed records for tax reporting.

Tax Reports:

- Generate essential tax reports such as Profit and Loss (P&L), Balance Sheet, and Income Tax Summary.
- Review these reports to understand your business's financial position and identify tax deductions.

Accountant Access:

- Invite your accountant or tax professional to collaborate on your QuickBooks Online account.
- Your accountant can access financial data, review transactions, and prepare tax returns.

Tax Compliance Features:

Tax Deadlines and Reminders:

- QBO provides reminders for tax filing deadlines, including sales tax, payroll taxes, and income taxes.
- Stay informed about upcoming tax obligations to avoid late filings and penalties.

Automatic Updates:

- QuickBooks Online updates tax rates, forms, and compliance requirements automatically.
- Ensure that your tax calculations remain accurate and up to date with the latest tax laws.

Compliance Checks:

- Run compliance checks within QBO to identify potential errors or discrepancies.
- The system flags issues related to missing information, incorrect tax rates, or incomplete forms.

Tax Deductions and Credits:

Expense Tracking:

- Categorize business expenses correctly to maximize tax deductions.
- Track deductible expenses such as office supplies, travel, rent, utilities, and more.

Mileage Tracking:

- Use the mileage tracking feature in QBO to record and calculate deductible business mileage.
- Ensure accurate records for mileage deductions at tax time.

Tax Support and Resources:

Help Center:

- QuickBooks Online offers a robust Help Center with tax-related articles, guides, and tutorials.
- Access resources on tax setup, compliance, deductions, and more.

Customer Support:

- If you have questions or need assistance with taxes in QBO, reach out to customer support.
- QBO support teams can provide guidance on tax setup, reporting, and compliance matters.

Bank Account Setup for Payroll

Setting up your bank account for payroll in QuickBooks Online (QBO) is an important step to ensure that employee paychecks are deposited accurately and on time. Here's a guide on how to set up your bank account for payroll:

Accessing Payroll Settings:

- Log in to your QuickBooks Online account.
- Navigate to the "Employees" or "Payroll" tab in the left-hand menu.

Setting Up Bank Account:

Click on "Payroll Settings" or "Bank Accounts":

- In the Payroll section, look for an option like "Payroll Settings" or "Bank Accounts" to manage your payroll bank account.

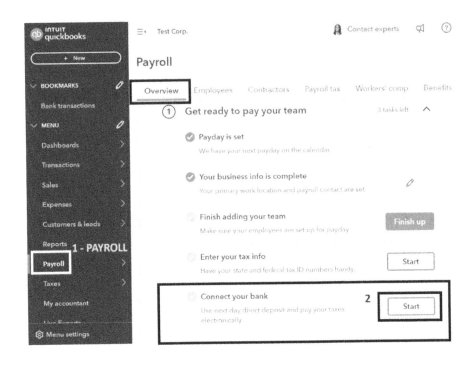

Add a New Bank Account:

- If you haven't set up a bank account for payroll yet, click on the option to add a new bank account.

Choose Account Type:

- Select the type of bank account you want to use for payroll. This could be a checking account or a specific payroll account.

Enter Bank Account Details:

- Enter the bank account details, including the account name, account number, and routing number.
- Verify the accuracy of the information to avoid any issues with payroll deposits.

Verify Test Transactions (Optional):

- QuickBooks may send test transactions to verify the account. Check your bank statements for these transactions.
- Log back into QuickBooks and enter the amounts of the test transactions to confirm your bank account.

Save Bank Account:

- Once you've entered all the necessary information and verified the account, save the bank account details.

Assigning Bank Account for Payroll:

Access Payroll Settings:

- In the Payroll section of QBO, find the option to manage payroll bank accounts.

Select Default Bank Account:

- Choose the bank account you just set up as the default account for payroll.
- This ensures that employee paychecks are deposited into this account by default.

Save Settings:

- Save the changes to apply the new bank account as the default for payroll.

Direct Deposit Setup (Optional):

Activate Direct Deposit (if not already done):

- If you plan to use direct deposit for employee paychecks, ensure that direct deposit is activated in your QBO account.

Employee Direct Deposit Setup:

- For each employee, set up their direct deposit details, including the bank account number and routing number.
- Employees can provide this information through secure channels within QBO or by filling out direct deposit authorization forms.

Verify Employee Direct Deposit Information:

- After entering employee direct deposit details, verify the accuracy of the information.
- Ensure that the correct bank account is selected for each employee.

Running Payroll:

Enter Employee Hours and Other Payroll Details:

- Before running payroll, enter employee hours, salaries, bonuses, deductions, and any other relevant payroll information.

Select Bank Account:

- When running payroll, choose the designated bank account for employee paychecks.
- This ensures that funds are withdrawn from the correct account and deposited into employees' accounts.

Process Payroll:

- Once you've reviewed and confirmed payroll details, process payroll.
- QuickBooks will calculate employee net pay, deductions, and taxes and create paychecks or direct deposit transactions.

Review transactions:

- After running payroll, review the transactions to ensure accuracy.
- Verify that employee paychecks are listed as withdrawals from the payroll bank account.

Record Transactions and Reconcile:

Record Payroll Transactions:

- QuickBooks automatically records payroll transactions, including employee wages, taxes, and deductions.
- These transactions appear in your bank register for the payroll bank account.

Reconcile Bank Statements:

- Regularly reconcile your bank statements with QuickBooks to ensure that payroll transactions match your bank records.
- This helps identify any discrepancies or errors in payroll deposits or withdrawals.

Bank Account Security:

Ensure Secure Access:

- Protect your QuickBooks account and bank account information with secure passwords and two-factor authentication.

Monitor Transactions:

- Regularly monitor your bank account for any unauthorized transactions.
- Notify your bank immediately if you notice any suspicious activity.

Running Your First Payroll

Running your first payroll in QuickBooks Online (QBO) involves a series of steps to ensure accurate calculations and timely payments to your employees. Here's a comprehensive guide to help you through the process:

Preparation:

Verify Employee Information:

- Make sure you have all necessary employee information on hand, including:
- Employee names, addresses, and Social Security Numbers (SSNs)
- Pay rates (hourly, salary, etc.)
- Withholding allowances
- Deductions (health insurance, retirement contributions, etc.)

Set Up Payroll Schedule:

- Determine your payroll schedule, whether it's weekly, bi-weekly, semi-monthly, or monthly.
- This will dictate how often you run payroll and when employees receive their pay.

Activate Payroll:

- If you haven't already, make sure your QuickBooks Online account is subscribed to a payroll plan.
- Activate the payroll feature in your account settings.

Entering Employee Hours:

Navigate to "Employees" or "Payroll":

- Log in to your QuickBooks Online account.
- Go to the "Employees" or "Payroll" tab in the left-hand menu.

Select "Run Payroll":

- Look for an option to "Run Payroll" or "Create Paychecks."
- Click on this option to begin the payroll process.

Enter Employee Hours:

- For each employee, enter the hours worked for the pay period.
- If you have salaried employees, you may not need to enter hours.

Review and Verify:

- Double-check the entered hours to ensure accuracy.
- Verify any overtime hours, if applicable.

Add Additional Earnings and Deductions:

Add Bonuses or Commissions:

- If employees are eligible for bonuses, commissions, or other additional earnings, enter these amounts.

Deductions and Contributions:

- Enter any deductions such as health insurance premiums, retirement plan contributions, or other employee contributions.
- Verify the accuracy of deduction amounts.

Preview and Confirm Payroll:

Check Payroll Summary:

- QuickBooks will generate a summary of the payroll, including total wages, deductions, and net pay for each employee.
- Review this summary carefully to ensure accuracy.

Make Adjustments (if needed):

- If you need to make any changes, go back to the employee's details and adjust as necessary.
- Verify that all changes are reflected correctly in the payroll summary.

Confirm Payroll:

- Once you're satisfied with the payroll details, click on the option to "Submit," "Approve," or "Finalize" payroll.
- This action confirms that you're ready to process the payroll.

Process Payroll:

Generate Paychecks or Direct Deposits:

- QuickBooks will now calculate each employee's net pay, deductions, and taxes.
- You can choose to print paychecks or process direct deposits based on your preferences.

Printing Paychecks:

- If you're printing paychecks, ensure you have enough check stock in your printer.
- Follow the on-screen prompts to print the paychecks.

Processing Direct Deposits:

- For direct deposit, QuickBooks will generate ACH files for each employee's bank account.
- Verify the bank account information and submit the ACH files to your bank for processing.

Record Payroll Transactions:

Recording in QuickBooks:

- QuickBooks will automatically record the payroll transactions for each employee.
- These transactions will include wages, taxes withheld, and any deductions.

Review Transactions:

- After processing payroll, review the transactions in your QuickBooks account.
- Ensure that each transaction is accurately recorded.

Payroll Reports and Compliance:

Generate Payroll Reports:

- QuickBooks offers various payroll reports that provide detailed insights into your payroll expenses.
- Run reports such as Payroll Summary, Payroll Details, and Payroll Tax Summary.

Tax Compliance:

- QBO automatically calculates and withholds federal, state, and local payroll taxes.
- Verify that taxes are withheld correctly based on employee information and tax tables.

Tax Filings and Payments:

- Keep track of tax filing deadlines and requirements for your jurisdiction.
- QuickBooks can generate and file tax forms such as W-2s, 1099s, and quarterly tax returns.

Employee Paystubs:

Accessing Paystubs:

- Employees can access their paystubs online through the QuickBooks Workforce portal.
- Invite employees to set up their QuickBooks Workforce accounts to view paystubs, tax forms, and other payroll-related information.

Sending Paystubs:

- If desired, you can also email or print paystubs for distribution to employees.
- QuickBooks provides options to email paystubs directly from the system.

Reconciliation and Review:

Reconcile Bank Statements:

- Reconcile your bank account to ensure that payroll transactions match your bank records.
- Compare the transactions in QuickBooks with your bank statement for accuracy.

Review for Accuracy:

- Periodically review your payroll records and reports to ensure accuracy and compliance.
- Make any necessary adjustments or corrections as needed.

Managing Employee Information and Payroll Taxes

Understanding and Managing Payroll Taxes

Understanding and managing payroll taxes in QuickBooks Online (QBO) is essential for every business to ensure compliance with tax regulations and avoid penalties. Here's a comprehensive guide to help you navigate payroll taxes in QBO:

Types of Payroll Taxes:

1. Employee Taxes:

- Federal Income Tax: Deducted from employee wages based on their W-4 form and tax brackets.

https://www.irs.gov/pub/irs-pdf/fw4.pdf

- State Income Tax: Deducted for employees in states with income tax.

FICA Taxes:

- **Social Security Tax:** 6.2% of employee wages up to a certain annual limit.
- **Medicare Tax:** 1.45% of all employee wages.

Additional Medicare tax for high-income earners (0.9% for wages over $200,000).

- **State Disability Insurance (SDI):** Required in some states for disability insurance programs.
- **Local Taxes:** Some cities or municipalities may have additional local income taxes.

Employer Taxes:

FICA Taxes:

- Employer's Share of Social Security: 6.2% of employee wages up to the annual limit.
- Employer's Share of Medicare: 1.45% of all employee wages.
- Federal Unemployment Tax (FUTA): 6% of the first $7,000 paid to each employee.
- State Unemployment Tax (SUTA): Varies by state, based on employee wages and the employer's unemployment history.

Setting Up Payroll Tax Items in QBO:

Navigate to Payroll Settings:

- Log in to your QBO account and go to the "Employees" or "Payroll" tab.
- Select "Payroll Settings" or "Payroll Tax" to set up tax items.

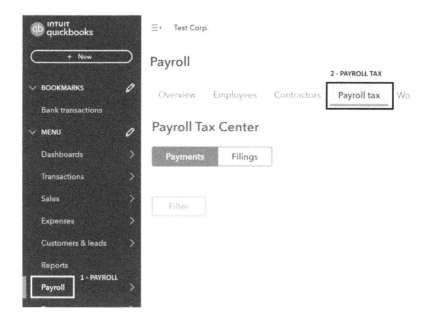

Add Tax Items:

- Click on "Add a new tax" or "Add tax" to create new payroll tax items.
- Choose the appropriate tax type (e.g., Federal Income Tax, State Income Tax, FICA Taxes, etc.).

Enter Tax Rates:

- Enter the tax rates for each tax item based on federal, state, and local tax regulations.
- QuickBooks will calculate these taxes automatically for each paycheck.

Employee Setup and Withholding:

Employee Information:

- Ensure all employee details are accurately entered in QBO, including their W-4 information.

- This includes filing status, allowances, additional withholding amounts, etc.

Withholding Calculations:

- QBO will calculate federal and state income tax withholdings based on the employee's W-4 information and tax rates.

Payroll Deductions:

- Deduct FICA taxes (Social Security and Medicare) from each paycheck based on employee wages.

Processing Payroll and Tax Calculation:

Run Payroll:

- When you run payroll in QBO, the system will calculate employee and employer taxes automatically.
- Verify the calculated amounts for each employee before finalizing payroll.

Verify Tax Withholdings:

- Review each employee's paycheck to ensure that the correct federal, state, and FICA taxes are withheld.
- QuickBooks provides detailed breakdowns of tax withholdings for each paycheck.

Employer Contributions:

- QuickBooks also calculates and tracks employer contributions for FICA taxes (Social Security and Medicare) and unemployment taxes.
- These amounts are recorded as payroll liabilities until they are paid.

Payroll Tax Payments:

Schedule Tax Payments:

- QBO provides reminders for upcoming tax payment due dates.
- Schedule payments for federal, state, and local payroll taxes through the system.

E-Payments:

- QBO allows you to make electronic federal tax payments (EFTPS) directly from the platform.
- Set up your bank account for electronic payments and authorize QBO to make payments on your behalf.

State Tax Payments:

- Some states also allow for electronic state tax payments through QuickBooks Online.
- Check with your state tax agency for available options and setup instructions.

Tax Forms and Filings:

Generate Tax Forms:

- QBO generates and files tax forms such as W-2s for employees and 941s for federal payroll taxes.
- These forms can be accessed, reviewed, and filed directly from the system.

Year-End Forms:

- At the end of the year, QuickBooks will generate and distribute W-2 forms to employees.
- File copies of W-2s, 1099s, and other year-end forms with the appropriate tax agencies.

Review and Reconciliation:

Payroll Reports:

- Run payroll reports in QBO to review tax withholdings, employer contributions, and payroll expenses.
- Reports such as Payroll Summary, Tax Liability, and Payroll Details provide valuable insights.

Bank Reconciliation:

- Reconcile your payroll bank account in QBO to ensure that payroll tax payments match your bank records.
- Compare payroll liabilities in QBO with actual payments made.

Seek Professional Advice:

Tax Advisor Consultation:

- If you're unsure about tax calculations, compliance, or deductions, consult with a tax advisor.
- A tax professional can provide personalized advice based on your business's specific situation.

QBO Support:

- QuickBooks Online offers support resources, including articles, tutorials, and customer service assistance.
- Reach out to QBO support for help with payroll tax setup, calculations, and reporting.

Running Payroll in QuickBooks Online

Step 1: Activate Payroll

- **Log In and Access Payroll Settings:**
  - Sign in to your QBO account.
  - Navigate to the "Employees" or "Payroll" tab and click on "Get Started" or "Turn on Payroll" to activate the feature.

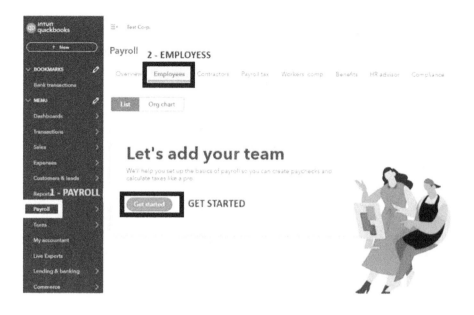

Step 2: Enter Company Information

- **Company Details:**
  - Input your company's legal name, address, Employer Identification Number (EIN), and contact details.
- **State Registration:**
  - Provide state tax registration details, including state tax ID numbers and withholding rates.

Step 3: Bank Account Setup

- **Add Payment Bank Account:**
  - Enter the bank account information from which employee payments and payroll taxes will be disbursed.

Step 4: Set Up Employees

- **Employee Information:**
  - Add details for each employee, such as name, address, Social Security Number (SSN), and tax withholding information from the W-4 form.

- **Pay Details:**
  - o Specify pay rates (hourly or salary), pay schedules, and start dates.

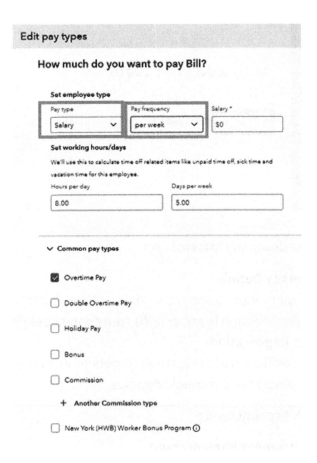

Step 5: Enter Payroll Items

- Earnings and Deductions:
  - o Set up earnings items like regular pay, overtime, and bonuses.
  - o Add deduction items for premiums, retirement contributions, etc.

- **Employer Contributions:**
  - Include employer contributions such as health insurance or retirement plans.

Step 6: Direct Deposit Setup (Optional)

- **Activate and Obtain Authorization:**
  - Set up direct deposit by entering bank details and obtaining authorization forms from employees.

Step 7: Define Payroll Schedule

- **Pay Frequencies and Processing Dates:**
  - Determine how often payroll will be run (e.g., weekly, bi-weekly) and establish processing dates to ensure timely payments.

Step 8: Review, Test, and Confirm Setup

- **Verify and Test Payroll:**
  - Double-check all employee details and run a test payroll to ensure everything calculates correctly.
- **Save and Confirm Activation:**
  - Save your payroll setup and confirm activation with QuickBooks.

Step 9: Run Your First Payroll

- **Start Payroll Run:**
  - Navigate to the "Employees" or "Payroll" tab and click "Run Payroll" or "Create Paychecks."
- Enter Hours and Review:
  - Input hours worked, additional earnings, and verify all details are accurate.
- **Generate Paychecks or Direct Deposit**:
  - Decide between printing checks or processing direct deposits. QuickBooks will handle tax calculations and deductions.

Step 10: Record and Monitor Payroll

- **Automatic Recording:**
  - o QuickBooks automatically records payroll transactions, including wages, taxes, and deductions.
- **Review Transactions and Confirm:**
  - o Ensure that all payroll entries are accurate and confirm the records in QuickBooks.

Step 11: Handle Tax Payments and Filings

- **Schedule and E-Payments:**
  - o Set reminders for tax payment due dates and use QuickBooks to make electronic federal and state tax payments as necessary.

Step 12: Compliance and Documentation

- **Distribute Pay Stubs and Communicate:**
  - o Provide pay stubs to employees and inform them of payment dates and how to access their pay details online.
- **Backup and Record Keeping:**
  - o Maintain and back up payroll records according to IRS guidelines and ensure all payroll data is secure and accessible.

By following this integrated guide, you will efficiently manage payroll setup and processing in QuickBooks Online, ensuring accuracy, compliance, and satisfaction for both the business and its employees.

CHAPTER 6
TAXES AND COMPLIANCE

Navigating Sales Tax Setup and Reporting

Introduction to Sales Tax in QBO

Sales tax in QuickBooks Online (QBO) is a crucial aspect of managing your business finances, especially if you sell taxable products or services. Here's an introduction to sales tax in QBO and how to set it up:

What is Sales Tax?

It is a tax imposed by the government on the sale of goods and services. Businesses collect sales tax from customers at the point of sale and remit it to the appropriate tax authority.

Setting Up Sales Tax in QuickBooks Online:

Activate Sales Tax Feature:

- Log in to your QuickBooks Online account.
- Navigate to the "Taxes" or "Sales Tax" tab in the left-hand menu (depending on your version).

- Click on "Set up sales tax" or "Get started" to activate the sales tax feature.

Enter Business Information:

- Provide your business's legal name, address, and tax identification number (TIN/EIN).
- Choose the tax filing frequency (monthly, quarterly, annually) based on your business's sales volume.

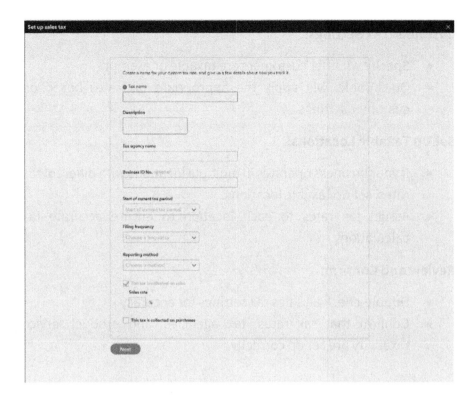

Set Up Sales Tax Agencies:

- Add the tax agencies to which you'll remit sales tax.
- QuickBooks will automatically calculate and track sales tax for each agency.

Define Tax Rates:

- Enter the sales tax rates applicable to your business.
- Rates may vary based on your location (state, county, city) and the types of products or services you sell.

Assign Tax Codes to Products/Services:

- Set up tax codes for each product or service you offer.
- Indicate whether each item is taxable or exempt from sales tax.

Customer Tax Settings:

- Specify whether customers are taxable or exempt.
- QuickBooks will apply the appropriate tax rates based on customer settings.

Set Up Taxable Locations:

- If your business operates in multiple locations with different tax rates, set up taxable locations.
- Assign tax rates to each location to ensure accurate tax calculations.

Review and Confirm:

- Double-check all sales tax settings for accuracy.
- Confirm that tax rates, tax agencies, and product/service taxability are set up correctly.

How QuickBooks Online Handles Sales Tax:

- **Automated Calculations:** QuickBooks automatically calculates sales tax on invoices, sales receipts, and other transactions based on your settings.
- **Tax-Inclusive Pricing:** You can set prices to include sales tax, and QuickBooks will calculate the tax amount for each sale.
- **Tax Tracking:** QuickBooks tracks sales tax amounts collected for each tax agency, making it easier to prepare and file tax returns.
- **Reporting:** Access sales tax reports to view tax collected by jurisdiction, taxable sales, and tax liabilities.
- **Remittance:** QuickBooks helps you prepare and file sales tax returns directly within the platform.
- **Reminders:** Receive reminders for upcoming tax due dates and filings to stay compliant.

Managing Sales Tax Transactions:

Create Sales Transactions:

- When creating invoices or sales receipts, QuickBooks will automatically calculate sales tax based on the customer's location and the item's tax code.

View Tax Amounts:

- Review the tax amount for each transaction before finalizing.
- QuickBooks displays the taxable amount, tax rate, and total tax calculated.

Track Taxable Sales:

- QuickBooks categorizes taxable sales separately in reports, making it easy to see total sales subject to tax.

Monitor Tax Liabilities:

- Access the Sales Tax Liability report to view the total tax collected and owed to each tax agency.
- QuickBooks tracks tax liabilities as you make sales and collect tax.

Prepare and File Tax Returns:

- QuickBooks can generate sales tax reports for each tax period.
- Use these reports to prepare and file sales tax returns with the appropriate tax agencies.

Record Tax Payments:

- When you remit sales tax payments to tax agencies, record these payments in QuickBooks.
- This ensures accurate tracking of tax liabilities and payments.

Sales Tax Compliance Tips:

- **Stay Updated:** Keep track of changes in sales tax rates and regulations. Collect Exemption Certificates: Maintain records of customers who are exempt from sales tax and their exemption certificates.
- **File on Time:** Adhere to the filing frequency (monthly, quarterly, annually) and deadlines for sales tax returns.
- **Audit Trails:** Keep detailed records of sales transactions, tax calculations, and payments for audit purposes.
- **Consult a Professional:** If you're unsure about sales tax requirements or calculations, seek advice from a tax professional.

Setting Up Sales Tax

Setting up sales tax in QuickBooks Online (QBO) is crucial for businesses that sell taxable products or services. Here's a step-by-step guide to help you set up sales tax in QBO:

Activate Sales Tax Feature:

- Log in to your QuickBooks Online account.
- Navigate to the "Taxes" or "Sales Tax" tab in the left-hand menu.
- Click on "Set up sales tax" or "Get started" to activate the sales tax feature.

Enter Business Information:

- Provide your business's legal name, address, and tax identification number (TIN/EIN).
- Choose the tax filing frequency (monthly, quarterly, annually) based on your business's sales volume.

Add Tax Agencies:

- Click on "Add agency" or "Add tax" to set up tax agencies to which you'll remit sales tax.

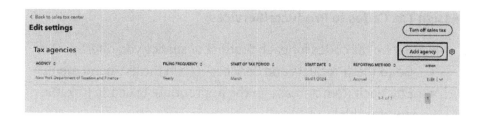

- Enter the names of the tax agencies (e.g., State Department of Revenue, Local Tax Authority).

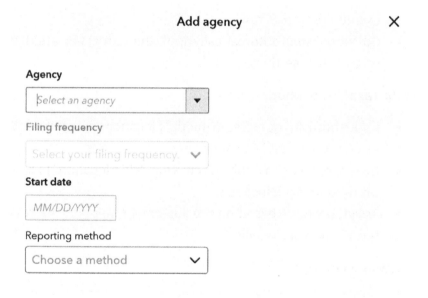

Define Tax Rates:

- Click on "Add rate" or "New" to enter the sales tax rates applicable to your business.
- Specify the tax rates for each agency, including state, county, city, or other jurisdictions.
- You can add multiple tax rates if your business operates in different locations with varying tax rates.

Assign Tax Codes to Products/Services:

- Set up tax codes for each product or service you offer.
- Go to the "Products and Services" tab in the left-hand menu.
- Edit each item and assign the appropriate tax code (taxable or non-taxable).

Set Customer Tax Settings:

- Go to the "Sales" or "Customers" tab in the left-hand menu.
- Edit customer profiles and specify whether they are taxable or exempt from sales tax.
- QuickBooks will automatically apply the correct tax rates based on customer settings.

Set Up Taxable Locations:

- If your business operates in multiple locations with different tax rates, set up taxable locations.
- Go to the "Sales Tax" tab and click on "Add a location" to specify tax rates for each location.
- Assign tax rates based on the customer's shipping address or the location of the sale.

Review and Confirm:

- Double-check all sales tax settings for accuracy.
- Confirm that tax rates, tax agencies, product/service taxability, and customer settings are set up correctly.

After Setting Up Sales Tax:

- **Create Sales Transactions:** When creating invoices or sales receipts, QuickBooks will automatically calculate sales tax based on your settings.
- **Review Tax Amounts:** Before finalizing transactions, review the tax amount for accuracy.

- **Track Taxable Sales:** QuickBooks categorizes taxable sales separately in reports, making it easy to see total sales subject to tax.
- **Prepare Tax Returns:** Use QuickBooks reports to prepare and file sales tax returns with the appropriate tax agencies.

Additional Considerations:

- **Tax on Expenses:** You can also set up sales tax on expenses by marking vendors as taxable.
- **Taxable Services:** If your business offers services subject to sales tax, ensure you've set up the appropriate tax codes.
- **Tax-Exempt Customers:** For customers who are exempt from sales tax, make sure to mark them as tax-exempt in their customer profile.

Managing Sales Tax Categories and Products

Managing sales tax categories and products in QuickBooks Online (QBO) involves setting up tax codes for your products or services and assigning the appropriate tax rates. Here's how you can manage sales tax categories and products in QBO:

Setting Up Sales Tax Categories:

- Sales tax categories help you organize your products or services based on their taxability. You can create different categories for taxable and non-taxable items.

Navigate to Products and Services:

- Log in to your QuickBooks Online account.
- Go to the "Sales" or "Sales and Products/Services" tab in the left-hand menu.
- Select "Products and Services" to view your list of items.

Create Sales Tax Categories:

- Click on the "New" button to add a new product or service.

- Under the "Category" field, create categories such as "Taxable" and "Non-Taxable."

- You can also create more specific categories based on your business needs (e.g., "Clothing Taxable," "Food Non-Taxable").

Assigning Tax Codes to Products/Services:

- Tax codes indicate whether an item is taxable or non-taxable. You'll need to assign the appropriate tax code to each product or service you offer.

Edit Existing Products/Services:

- In the "Products and Services" list, locate the item you want to edit.
- Click on the item to open its details.

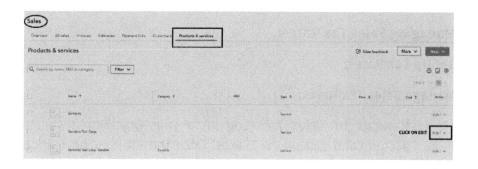

Assign Tax Codes:

- In the item details, find the "Sales tax category" or "Taxable" field.
- Select the appropriate category or tax code from the dropdown menu.
- Choose "Taxable" for items subject to sales tax and "Non-Taxable" for exempt items.

Setting Up Taxable and Non-Taxable Products:

Taxable Products/Services:

- For items subject to sales tax, select the "Taxable" category or tax code.
- Enter the appropriate sales tax rate based on your business location and tax jurisdiction.

Non-Taxable Products/Services:

- For items that are exempt from sales tax, select the "Non-Taxable" category or tax code.
- No sales tax will be applied to transactions involving these items.

Managing Sales Tax Rates:

Set Up Tax Rates:

Manage Sales Tax Rates:

- Navigate to Taxes Tab: Log in to your QuickBooks Online account and click on the "Taxes" tab in the left-hand navigation menu.
- Select Sales Tax: Within the Taxes tab, click on "Sales tax."
- Manage Tax Rates: You'll see a list of your existing sales tax rates. To manage them, you can edit, deactivate, or add new tax rates as needed.
- Edit Tax Rates: To edit a tax rate, simply click on the tax rate you want to modify, make the necessary changes, and then click "Save."
- Deactivate Tax Rates: If you no longer need a tax rate, you can deactivate it by clicking on the tax rate and then selecting "Deactivate" from the options.
- Add New Tax Rates: To add a new tax rate, click on the "Add tax" button. Fill in the required information, such as the tax name, agency, rate, and effective date, then click "Save."

Specify Tax Rates:

- Navigate to Sales Settings: Click on the "Settings" icon (gear icon) in the top-right corner of the QuickBooks Online window, then select "Account and Settings" or "Company Settings."
- Go to Sales Settings: Within the Account and Settings or Company Settings menu, click on "Sales" or "Sales settings."
- Enable Sales Tax: Make sure the sales tax feature is enabled. If it's not already enabled, toggle the switch to turn it on.
- Specify Tax Rates: Scroll down to the section where you can specify default tax rates. Here, you can choose the default tax agency and tax rate for your sales transactions.
- Save Changes: After specifying the default tax rates, make sure to click "Save" to apply your changes.

Review and Update:

Regularly Review:

- Periodically review your products/services list to ensure all items have the correct tax codes.
- Update tax codes as needed for new products, changes in tax laws, or adjustments to tax rates.

Edit Product Details:

- To edit product details, go to the "Products and Services" list.
- Click on the item you want to edit, then update the "Sales tax category" or tax code.

Creating New Products/Services:

Add New Items:

- To add a new product or service, click on the "New" button in the "Products and Services" list.
- Enter the item details, including the name, description, price, and sales tax category.

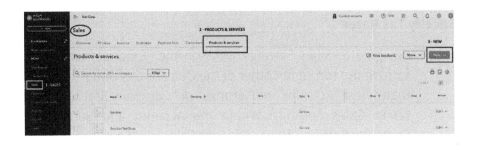

Assign Tax Codes:

- Choose the appropriate sales tax category or tax code for the new item.
- Save the changes to add the item to your products/services list.

Reporting and Tracking:

Sales Tax Reports:

- Use QuickBooks' sales tax reports to track tax collected, taxable sales, and tax liabilities.
- Generate reports such as "Sales Tax Liability" and "Taxable Sales Detail" to monitor sales tax activities.

Sales Tax Liability:

- This report shows the total sales tax collected for each tax agency.
- It also displays the amount you owe to each agency for a specific period.

Best Practices:

- **Regular Updates:** Keep your products/services list up to date with accurate tax codes.
- **Double-check New Items:** When adding new products/ services, ensure the correct tax category or code is selected.

- **Review Reports:** Regularly review sales tax reports to reconcile tax collected and ensure accuracy.
- **Stay Informed:** Stay informed about changes in tax rates or regulations that may affect your business.

Preparing for Year-End Taxes and Filings

Introduction to Year-End Tax Preparation

Preparing for year-end tax activities in QuickBooks Online (QBO) involves several crucial steps to ensure accurate financial records and smooth tax filing. Here's an introduction to year-end tax preparation in QBO:

Review Financial Records:

Income and Expenses:

- Review your income and expense transactions for the year.
- Ensure all transactions are categorized correctly.

Bank Reconciliation:

- Reconcile your bank and credit card accounts to ensure they match your records.
- Address any discrepancies or outstanding transactions.

Verify Employee and Vendor Information:

Employee Details:

- Ensure all employee information is up to date, including names, addresses, Social Security Numbers (SSNs), and tax withholding details.

Vendor Information:

- Verify vendor details, including names, addresses, Tax Identification Numbers (TINs), and payment amounts.

Complete Payroll Tasks:

Payroll Reconciliation:

- Reconcile your payroll transactions to ensure they align with your payroll reports.

Employee Benefits:

- Review and confirm employee benefits, such as health insurance premiums and retirement contributions.

Year-End Bonuses:

- Process any year-end bonuses or additional compensation for employees.

Prepare for 1099s:

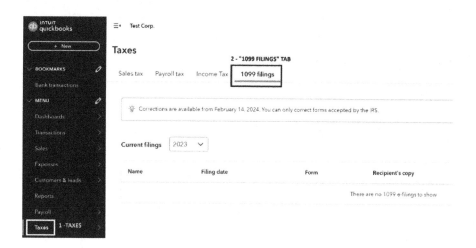

Vendor Payments:

- Identify vendors who need to receive a 1099 form for the year.

Confirm TINs:

- Verify Tax Identification Numbers (TINs) for each vendor.

Generate 1099s:

- Use QuickBooks Online to generate and distribute 1099 forms to applicable vendors.

Close the Books for the Year:

Adjust Entries:

- Make any necessary adjusting entries to reflect year-end adjustments.

Depreciation and Amortization:

- Record depreciation and amortization expenses for fixed assets.

Accruals and Deferrals:

- Address any accruals or deferrals for expenses or revenue.

Run Year-End Reports:

Profit and Loss (P&L):

- Generate a P&L report for the year to review your business's profitability.

Balance Sheet:

- Review your balance sheet to see your business's financial position.

Tax Reports:

- Use QuickBooks' tax reports, such as the Tax Summary report, to assist with tax preparation.

Prepare for Tax Filings:

Organize Documents:

- Gather necessary tax documents, such as W-2s, 1099s, and receipts.

Tax Deductions:

- Review potential tax deductions for your business, such as business expenses and charitable contributions.

Estimate Tax Liability:

- Use tax reports and financial records to estimate your business's tax liability for the year.

Check for Tax Law Changes:

Stay Informed:

- Stay up to date with any changes in tax laws that may affect your business.

Consult Professionals:

- Consider consulting with a tax professional or accountant for guidance on tax planning.

File Year-End Tax Returns:

Federal Taxes:

- Prepare and file your federal income tax return using the information gathered.

State and Local Taxes:

- File state and local tax returns based on your business location(s) and operations.

Generate and Distribute Employee W-2s:

W-2 Forms:

- Use QuickBooks Online to generate W-2 forms for each employee.

Employee Distribution:

- Provide employees with their W-2 forms by January 31st of the following year.

Review Tax Filing Deadlines:

Federal Deadlines:

- Verify the deadline for filing federal tax returns, typically April 15th, unless extended.

State and Local Deadlines:

- Check the deadlines for filing state and local tax returns, as they may vary.

Store Year-End Documents:

Document Retention:

- Keep copies of all tax documents, financial records, and year-end reports.

Electronic Storage:

- Consider using cloud storage or digital filing systems for easy access and organization.

Plan for Next Year:

Tax Planning:

- Develop a tax planning strategy for the upcoming year based on current financial data.

Budgeting:

- Create a budget for the new year to guide your business's financial decisions.

Organizing Financial Records

Organizing financial records in QuickBooks Online (QBO) is essential for maintaining accurate and up-to-date financial information. Here are some steps to help you organize your financial records effectively:

Set Up Proper Chart of Accounts:

Understand Chart of Accounts:

- The Chart of Accounts is a list of all accounts used by your business to classify transactions.
- It includes categories such as assets, liabilities, equity, income, and expenses.

Customize Accounts:

- Tailor your Chart of Accounts to fit your business needs.
- Add specific accounts for different income sources, expenses, assets, and liabilities.

Use Sub-Accounts:

- Create sub-accounts to further categorize transactions within main account categories.
- For example, under "Utilities Expense," you could have sub-accounts for electricity, water, and gas.

Consistently Categorize Transactions:

Assign Correct Categories:

- When entering transactions, ensure they are categorized correctly.
- Assign income transactions to the appropriate income account and expenses to the correct expense account.

Use Bank Rules:

- Create bank rules to automatically categorize recurring transactions.
- QuickBooks will apply these rules to future transactions, saving time and ensuring consistency.

Reconcile Bank and Credit Card Accounts:

Regular Reconciliation:

- Reconcile your bank and credit card accounts regularly to ensure accuracy.
- Match transactions in QuickBooks to statements from your financial institutions.

Address Discrepancies:

- Investigate and resolve any discrepancies between QuickBooks records and bank statements.
- This helps maintain the accuracy of your financial data.

Attach and Organize Documents:

Document Attachments:

- Use QuickBooks' document attachment feature to attach receipts, invoices, and other financial documents to transactions.
- This provides a clear record of supporting documents for each transaction.

Organize Attachments:

- Create folders or categories for document attachments within QuickBooks.
- This makes it easy to locate and access specific documents when needed.

Maintain Customer and Vendor Details:

Complete Profiles:

- Ensure customer and vendor profiles are complete and up to date.
- Include contact information, payment terms, and any specific details relevant to each customer or vendor.

Use Customer and Vendor Types:

- Create customer and vendor types to group similar customers/ vendors together.
- This helps in analyzing sales trends and managing vendor relationships.

Track Inventory (If Applicable):

Set Up Inventory Items:

- If your business sells products, set up inventory items in QuickBooks.
- Assign each item a SKU, description, cost, selling price, and quantity on hand.

Monitor Inventory Levels:

- Regularly update inventory quantities to reflect purchases and sales.
- Use inventory reports to track stock levels and reorder when necessary.

Generate and Review Reports:

Financial Statements:

- Run financial reports such as Profit and Loss (Income Statement) and Balance Sheet.

- Analyze these reports to understand your business's financial health and performance.

Custom Reports:

- Create custom reports to track specific metrics or KPIs relevant to your business.
- Use these reports for budgeting, forecasting, and decision-making.

Use Classes or Locations (If Needed):

Organize by Classes:

- Use Classes to categorize transactions by departments, locations, or projects.
- This allows for segmented reporting and analysis.

Track by Locations:

- If your business operates in multiple locations, use Locations to track income and expenses by location.
- This helps in understanding profitability and performance across different branches.

Backup Data Regularly:

Data Security:

- Protect your financial data by regularly backing up QuickBooks Online.
- QuickBooks provides automatic backups, but you can also manually create backups for added security.

Store Backups Safely:

- Store backup files in secure locations, such as cloud storage or external hard drives.

- Ensure backups are accessible in case of data loss or system failure.

Consult with Professionals:

Tax Advisors:

- Work with tax advisors or accountants to ensure compliance with tax laws and regulations.
- They can provide guidance on tax planning, deductions, and filings.

QuickBooks Experts:

- Consult with QuickBooks ProAdvisors or experts for help with advanced features and troubleshooting.
- They can provide training and assistance tailored to your business needs.

Maximizing Deductions and Credits

Maximizing deductions and credits in QuickBooks Online (QBO) can help reduce your taxable income and save your business money. Here are some strategies to help you make the most of deductions and credits in QuickBooks:

Accurate Expense Tracking:

Categorize Expenses:

- Ensure all business expenses are categorized correctly in QuickBooks.
- Use specific accounts for different types of expenses (e.g., office supplies, utilities, travel).

Attach Receipts:

- Attach receipts or invoices to expense transactions in QuickBooks.
- This provides supporting documentation for deductions during tax time.

Employee Expenses:

Reimbursements:

- Record employee expenses and reimbursements accurately in QuickBooks.
- Use "Reimbursable Expenses" or "Billable Expenses" features to track and bill clients for reimbursed expenses.

Mileage Tracking:

- Use QuickBooks' mileage tracking feature to record business-related mileage.
- The IRS standard mileage rate is a deductible expense for business travel.

Home Office Deduction:

Set Up Home Office:

- If you have a home office, ensure it meets IRS requirements for the home office deduction.
- Calculate the percentage of your home used for business and enter it in QuickBooks.

Record Home Office Expenses:

- Deductible expenses include a portion of your rent or mortgage interest, utilities, insurance, and maintenance.
- Record these expenses in QuickBooks with appropriate accounts and categories.

Business Use of Vehicle:

Track Mileage:

- Use QuickBooks' mileage tracking feature to log business-related vehicle mileage.
- This includes travel to client meetings, job sites, and other business-related trips.

Actual Expenses vs. Mileage Rate:

- Compare the standard mileage rate (set by the IRS) with actual vehicle expenses.
- Deduct the higher of the two methods for vehicle expenses.

Equipment and Asset Purchases:

Section 179 Deduction:

- Take advantage of the Section 179 deduction for equipment and asset purchases.
- QuickBooks can help track these purchases and calculate depreciation.

Bonus Depreciation:

- Consider bonus depreciation for qualified property purchases.
- QuickBooks can help you track and apply these depreciation deductions.

Charitable Contributions:

Record Donations:

- Record all charitable contributions made by your business in QuickBooks.
- Ensure you have documentation (receipts, acknowledgments) for these donations.

Non-Cash Donations:

- If your business donates goods or services, record the fair market value in QuickBooks.
- Keep detailed records and descriptions of donated items.

Health Insurance Premiums:

Employer-Paid Premiums:

- Record employer-paid health insurance premiums as a business expense in QuickBooks.
- These premiums are fully deductible for self-employed individuals.

Employee Premiums:

- Track and deduct employee-paid health insurance premiums.
- QuickBooks can help you manage these deductions and benefits.

Retirement Contributions:

Employer Contributions:

- Record employer contributions to retirement plans, such as SEP-IRAs or 401(k)s.
- These contributions are deductible as business expenses.

Employee Contributions:

- Deduct employee contributions to retirement plans, such as Traditional IRAs or 401(k)s.
- Ensure accurate recording and reporting of these contributions in QuickBooks.

Research and Development Credits:

Qualifying Activities:

- If your business engages in research and development activities, you may qualify for R&D tax credits.
- Track and document R&D expenses in QuickBooks for potential deductions.

Work Opportunity Tax Credit (WOTC):

Hiring Credits:

- If you hire individuals from specific target groups (e.g., veterans, ex-felons, disabled individuals), you may qualify for WOTC.
- QuickBooks can help track employee hiring information to determine eligibility.

Education and Training Expenses:

Job-Related Education:

- Deduct expenses for job-related education, such as workshops, seminars, or certifications.
- Record these expenses in QuickBooks under the appropriate category.

Consult with Tax Professionals:

Tax Advisors:

- Work with tax advisors or accountants to maximize deductions and credits for your business.
- They can provide guidance on tax planning strategies and identify available tax breaks.

QuickBooks Experts:

- Consult with QuickBooks ProAdvisors or experts for help with utilizing QuickBooks features for tax purposes.
- They can provide training and advice on maximizing deductions within QuickBooks.

Review and Analyze Reports:

Tax Reports:

- Use QuickBooks' tax reports to review deductible expenses, credits, and deductions.
- Generate reports such as Profit and Loss, Tax Summary, and Expense Reports for analysis.

Year-End Review:

- Conduct a year-end review of your financial data to identify missed deductions or credits.
- Make any necessary adjustments or corrections in QuickBooks before tax filing.

Utilizing QuickBooks Online for Tax Preparation

Utilizing QuickBooks Online (QBO) for tax preparation can streamline the process, ensure accuracy, and save you time when filing your business taxes. Here's how you can effectively use QuickBooks Online for tax preparation:

Organize and Review Financial Data:

Categorize Transactions:

- Ensure all income and expenses are categorized correctly in QuickBooks Online.
- Use specific accounts for different types of income, expenses, assets, and liabilities.

Reconcile Accounts:

- Regularly reconcile bank and credit card accounts to match your records with financial institution statements.
- Address any discrepancies or outstanding transactions.

Review Reports:

- Generate financial reports such as Profit and Loss (Income Statement) and Balance Sheet.
- Review these reports to understand your business's financial health and identify potential deductions.

Maximize Deductions:

Expense Tracking:

- Track all business-related expenses in QuickBooks Online.
- Ensure accurate categorization and recording of deductible expenses, such as office supplies, rent, utilities, and mileage.

Depreciation and Amortization:

- Utilize QuickBooks' tools to track and calculate depreciation for business assets.
- Take advantage of depreciation deductions for equipment, vehicles, and other assets.

Home Office Deduction:

- If you have a home office, use QuickBooks to calculate the home office deduction.
- Ensure you meet the IRS requirements and accurately record the square footage of your home office.

Employee Expenses:

- Record and track employee expenses, reimbursements, and benefits.

- Use QuickBooks' features to categorize and report these expenses for tax deductions.

Retirement Contributions:

- Record employer contributions to retirement plans, such as SEP-IRAs or 401(k)s.
- Track employee contributions for tax deductions and retirement planning.

Health Insurance Premiums:

- Record employer-paid health insurance premiums as a deductible business expense.
- Deduct employee-paid health insurance premiums from taxable income.

State and Local Taxes:

- Ensure QuickBooks accurately tracks and reports state and local taxes paid.
- Review state-specific tax deductions and credits for your business operations.

Generate Tax Reports:

Tax Summary Report:

- Use QuickBooks' Tax Summary report to review taxable income, deductions, and credits.
- This report provides an overview of your tax liability and helps identify potential areas for optimization.

Profit and Loss Detail:

- Review the Profit and Loss Detail report to analyze specific income and expense details.
- Identify any overlooked deductions or expenses that can reduce your taxable income.

Expense Reports:

- Generate detailed expense reports to substantiate deductions during tax audits.
- Customize reports to include specific expense categories or time periods.

Utilize Tax Tools and Features:

Tax Forms:

- QuickBooks Online offers a feature to generate tax forms directly from your financial data.
- Prepare and print tax forms such as W-2s, 1099s, and 941s for employees and contractors.

Tax Deduction Finder:

- Use QuickBooks' built-in tax deduction finder tool to identify potential deductions.
- This tool scans your transactions and suggests deductions based on your business activities.

Tax Calculator:

- QuickBooks' tax calculator estimates your tax liability based on your financial data.
- Use this feature for tax planning and forecasting throughout the year.

Prepare for Tax Filings:

Tax Filing Deadlines:

- Stay informed about federal, state, and local tax filing deadlines.
- Use QuickBooks' reminders and notifications to avoid missing important deadlines.

E-Filing:

- QuickBooks Online allows for direct e-filing of tax forms with the IRS and state tax agencies.
- Submit tax returns and payments electronically for faster processing and confirmation.

Export Data:

- If working with a tax professional, export financial data from QuickBooks for tax preparation.
- Export reports, tax forms, and transaction details in various formats for easy sharing.

Consult with Tax Professionals:

Tax Advisors:

- Work with tax advisors or accountants to review your QuickBooks data for tax optimization.
- They can provide guidance on tax planning strategies, deductions, and credits.

QuickBooks ProAdvisors:

- Consult with QuickBooks ProAdvisors for assistance with tax-specific features and reports.
- ProAdvisors can provide training and support tailored to your tax preparation needs.

Keep Records and Documentation:

Document Storage:

- Store all tax-related documents and receipts securely in QuickBooks Online.
- Use the document attachment feature to link receipts to expense transactions.

Record Retention:

- Keep copies of tax returns, financial reports, and supporting documents for several years.
- QuickBooks Online allows for easy access to historical data and reports.

Review Before Filing:

Final Check:

- Before filing your tax return, review all financial data, reports, and deductions in QuickBooks.
- Verify accuracy and completeness to avoid errors or omissions.

Tax Planning for Next Year:

- Use insights from this year's tax preparation to plan for the next tax year.
- Implement strategies for maximizing deductions and credits going forward.

Filing Your Taxes

Filing your taxes using QuickBooks Online (QBO) can streamline the process, ensure accuracy, and save you time during tax season. Here's a step-by-step guide to help you file your taxes in QuickBooks Online:

Prepare Your Financial Data:

Review Financial Reports:

- Generate essential financial reports such as Profit and Loss (Income Statement) and Balance Sheet.
- Ensure all income, expenses, deductions, and credits are accurately recorded in QuickBooks Online.

Verify Tax Information:

- Confirm that your business's legal name, address, Employer Identification Number (EIN), and other tax details are correct.
- Ensure employee and vendor information, including W-2s and 1099s, is up to date.

Generate Tax Reports:

Tax Summary Report:

- Run the Tax Summary report in QuickBooks Online to review your business's taxable income, deductions, and credits.
- This report provides an overview of your tax liability and helps identify potential areas for optimization.

Profit and Loss Detail:

- Review the Profit and Loss Detail report to analyze specific income and expense details for tax deductions.
- Identify any overlooked expenses that can reduce your taxable income.

Use Tax Tools and Features:

Tax Forms:

- QuickBooks Online allows you to generate tax forms directly from your financial data.
- Prepare and print tax forms such as W-2s, 1099s, 941s, and others for employees, contractors, and the IRS.

Tax Deduction Finder:

- Utilize QuickBooks' tax deduction finder tool to identify potential deductions based on your business activities.
- The tool scans your transactions and suggests deductions to reduce your tax liability.

Tax Calculator:

- QuickBooks' tax calculator estimates your tax liability based on your financial data.
- Use this feature for tax planning and forecasting throughout the year.

E-Filing Tax Forms:

Direct E-Filing:

- QuickBooks Online allows for direct e-filing of tax forms with the IRS and state tax agencies.
- Submit tax returns and payments electronically for faster processing and confirmation.

E-File Federal and State Taxes:

- E-file your federal tax return directly from QuickBooks Online.
- File state and local tax returns electronically, if applicable, using the corresponding tax forms.

Export Data for Tax Professionals:

Share Financial Data:

- If working with a tax professional or accountant, export your financial data from QuickBooks Online.
- Export reports, tax forms, transaction details, and other relevant data in various formats for easy sharing.

Collaboration:

- Collaborate with tax professionals by providing access to your QuickBooks Online account.
- They can review your financial data, prepare tax returns, and file taxes on your behalf.

Final Review and Submission:

Review Tax Return:

- Before filing your tax return, thoroughly review all financial data, reports, and deductions in QuickBooks Online.
- Verify accuracy, completeness, and compliance with tax laws.

Double-Check Information:

- Ensure all tax forms, schedules, and attachments are completed accurately.
- Verify that your business's tax identification number (EIN or Social Security Number) is correct.

Submit Tax Returns:

Federal Taxes:

- File your federal tax return directly through QuickBooks Online.
- Review the submission process, verify payment information, and submit your return.

State and Local Taxes:

- File state and local tax returns electronically, if applicable, using the corresponding tax forms.
- Follow the specific instructions for each jurisdiction, including payment methods and deadlines.

Record Tax Payments:

Record Tax Payments:

- After filing, record tax payments made to the IRS and state tax agencies.
- Use QuickBooks' "Record Tax Payment" feature to accurately track and categorize tax payments.

Update Transactions:

- Ensure tax payments are reflected in your financial records to avoid duplicate entries or errors.
- QuickBooks will automatically reconcile the payments with your bank transactions.

Document Retention:

Keep Records Secure:

- Maintain copies of all tax-related documents, financial reports, and tax returns for several years.
- Store these documents securely in QuickBooks Online or a designated folder for easy access.

Compliance:

- Comply with IRS guidelines for record retention to ensure you have documentation in case of an audit.
- QuickBooks Online provides secure storage and backup for your financial records.

Review Tax Filing Confirmation:

Confirmation Receipt:

- After filing your tax returns, confirm that you receive a filing confirmation from the IRS and state tax agencies.
- Check for any notifications or correspondence regarding your tax filings.

Follow Up:

- If you encounter any issues or discrepancies, follow up with the IRS or tax agencies promptly.
- Address any requests for additional information or corrections as needed.

CHAPTER 7
LEVERAGING ARTIFICIAL INTELLIGENCE WITH QUICKBOOKS ONLINE

Introduction to AI in QBO and Its Benefits

Intro and Key AI Features in QBO

QuickBooks Online (QBO) is an accounting software that offers a range of AI-powered features designed to simplify financial tasks, automate processes, and provide valuable insights for businesses of all sizes. Here's an introduction to QBO's key AI features:

Overview of QuickBooks Online:

- QuickBooks Online is a cloud-based accounting software that allows businesses to manage their finances efficiently. It offers a variety of tools and features to help businesses track income and expenses, create and send invoices, manage bills, track inventory, run reports, and more—all accessible from anywhere with an internet connection.

Benefits of AI Features in QuickBooks Online:

- **Time-Saving:** AI automates tedious tasks such as data entry, categorization, and report generation, saving valuable time for business owners and employees.
- **Accuracy and Efficiency:** AI-driven processes reduce the likelihood of human errors in financial transactions and calculations.
- **Insights and Analytics:** AI-generated reports and insights provide valuable data for strategic decision-making and business planning.
- **Cost Savings:** By streamlining processes and reducing manual labor, businesses can save on labor costs and improve overall efficiency.
- **Compliance and Security:** AI helps ensure compliance with tax laws, payroll regulations, and financial reporting standards.
- **Improved Customer and Vendor Relationships:** AI insights on customer preferences and vendor interactions can lead to better customer service and vendor management.

The Future of AI in QBO

The future of AI in QuickBooks Online (QBO) is set to revolutionize the way you manage your business finances. Advancements in AI technology are expected to bring sophisticated automation capabilities into your accounting tasks. Imagine AI handling entire accounting cycles—from recording transactions to preparing financial statements—minimizing the need for manual input and reducing errors. This will free up your time, allowing you to focus more on strategic business decisions.

You can also expect AI to deliver personalized financial insights that are tailored specifically to your business's patterns and needs. Whether it's offering budgeting advice, investment suggestions, or proactive alerts about potential cash flow shortfalls, AI's predictive analytics will help you make more informed decisions. Additionally, AI will be instrumental in ensuring that your business remains compliant with constantly evolving tax laws and financial regulations by automatically updating systems and processes in real time.

The interaction with QuickBooks Online is also expected to become more intuitive. Advanced AI-driven assistants capable of understanding and executing complex commands in natural language could become your personal financial advisors, helping you navigate through various financial decisions and functionalities seamlessly.

AI's integration won't stop at financial management—it extends to broader business operations such as inventory management, customer relationship management (CRM), and human resources. By analyzing data across platforms, AI could provide insights on optimizing pricing strategies or managing supply chain finances effectively.

Real-time decision-making support will be another major advancement. With AI, QuickBooks Online will be able to provide immediate analytics and support, enabling you to respond swiftly to financial opportunities or challenges as they arise. Moreover, AI will enhance the security features within QuickBooks Online, using continuous learning to detect and respond to potential security threats more effectively, ensuring that your sensitive financial data remains protected.

Although these features are still on the horizon, as AI continues to evolve, its integration into QuickBooks Online promises to deliver increasingly innovative solutions that cater to the dynamic needs of your business, helping you to navigate the complexities of financial management with greater ease and confidence.

Identifying Potential Customers

In QuickBooks Online (QBO), you can use various features and tools to identify potential customers and target your marketing efforts effectively. Here are some steps to help you identify potential customers in QBO:

Customer List Analysis:

Generate Customer Reports:

- Run customer reports in QuickBooks Online to analyze past sales and customer interactions.
- Go to "Reports" > "Custom reports" > "Customer Contact List" to view a list of all customers

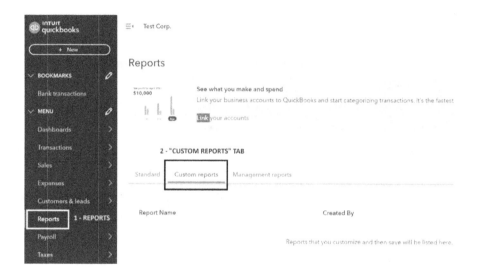

Sort and Filter Data:

- Sort customer lists by total sales, transaction frequency, or other relevant metrics.
- Use filters to segment customers by location, industry, purchase history, or other criteria.

Identify High-Value Customers:

- Identify customers who make frequent or high-value purchases.
- These customers are more likely to provide repeat business and referrals.

Review Sales Trends:

Sales by Product/Service:

- Analyze which products or services are most popular among your customers.
- Focus on promoting these offerings to potential customers who might be interested.

Seasonal Trends:

- Identify seasonal sales trends based on historical data.
- Plan targeted marketing campaigns or promotions during peak seasons.

Create Customer Groups or Segments:

Customer Types or Categories:

- Use customer types or categories to group similar customers together.
- For example, categorize customers as "Wholesale," "Retail," "New," or "VIP."

Customer Tags or Labels:

- Tag customers with specific attributes or interests.
- For instance, tag customers interested in a particular product line or service.

Utilize Contact Information:

Email Marketing:

- Export customer email lists from QuickBooks Online for email marketing campaigns.
- Send targeted promotions, newsletters, or updates to engage potential customers.

Follow-Up Calls or Emails:

- Reach out to customers who have inquired about products or services.
- Use QuickBooks' customer contact information to schedule follow-up calls or emails.

Customer Relationship Management (CRM) Integration:

Integrate with CRM Tools:

- Connect QuickBooks Online with CRM software to manage customer interactions.
- CRM tools like Salesforce, HubSpot, or Zoho CRM can track leads, contacts, and deals.

Track Interactions:

- Log customer interactions, inquiries, or purchases within the CRM.
- Use this information to nurture leads and build relationships with potential customers.

Lead Tracking and Conversion:

Sales Leads in QuickBooks:

- Use the "Leads" feature in QuickBooks Online to track potential customers.
- Record lead details, interactions, and follow-up actions.

Convert Leads to Customers:

- When leads show interest or intent to purchase, convert them into customers in QuickBooks.
- Track the conversion process and monitor customer engagement.

Website and Social Media Integration:

Capture Website Leads:

- Integrate QuickBooks Online with your website's lead capture forms.
- Automatically import leads into QuickBooks for follow-up.

Social Media Monitoring:

- Monitor social media channels for mentions, inquiries, or discussions about your business.
- Engage with potential customers and direct them to your products or services.

Tailoring Marketing Efforts with Precision

Tailoring marketing efforts with precision in QuickBooks Online (QBO) involves using its features to analyze customer data, create targeted campaigns, and track results for maximum impact. Here's how you can tailor your marketing efforts with precision in QBO:

Customer Segmentation:

Customer Types or Tags:

- Create customer types or tags based on demographics, interests, or buying behavior.
- Segment customers into groups such as "New Customers," "VIP Customers," "Preferred Products," etc.

Purchase History:

- Analyze customer purchase history in QBO.
- Identify patterns, preferences, and recurring purchases to tailor marketing offers.

Geographic Segmentation:

- Use customer addresses in QBO to segment by location.
- Target customers in specific regions with localized marketing campaigns.

Targeted Email Campaigns:

Customer Email Lists:

- Create email lists based on customer segments in QBO.
- Send personalized emails with targeted offers, promotions, or product recommendations.

Email Templates:

- Use QBO's email templates to create professional and branded emails.
- Customize templates with customer names, purchase history, and personalized messages.

Scheduled Emails:

- Schedule email campaigns in advance using QBO.
- Send emails at strategic times, such as holidays, anniversaries, or special events.

Promotions and Discounts:

Customer-Specific Offers:

- Offer exclusive promotions or discounts to specific customer segments.
- Create loyalty rewards for repeat customers or VIP members.

Coupon Codes and Special Deals:

- Generate unique coupon codes in QBO for targeted customer groups.

- Track coupon usage and redemption to measure campaign effectiveness.

Personalized Recommendations:

Product Recommendations:

- Use customer purchase history to recommend related or complementary products.
- Highlight new arrivals, best-sellers, or personalized product suggestions.

Cross-Selling and Upselling:

- Identify opportunities for cross-selling or upselling based on customer buying behavior.
- Offer bundled products, add-ons, or upgrades to enhance customer value.

Social Media Integration:

Social Media Ads:

- Integrate QBO with social media platforms for targeted advertising.
- Create custom audiences based on customer segments in QBO for precise ad targeting.

Social Media Engagement:

- Analyze customer interactions on social media linked to QBO.
- Respond to comments, messages, and reviews to build customer relationships.

Event Marketing:

Event Tracking:

- Record customer attendance at events or webinars in QBO.
- Follow up with attendees with targeted offers or follow-up emails.

Event Invitations:

- Create and send event invitations directly from QBO.
- Track RSVPs and attendee lists for event planning and follow-up.

Getting Started with AI in QBO

QuickBooks Online (QBO) incorporates several AI and machine learning features that are currently in use, enhancing various aspects of financial management. Here are some of the key AI features already implemented in QBO:

- **Automated Transaction Categorization**: QBO uses machine learning to automatically categorize bank transactions based on historical data and patterns. This feature helps to save time and increase accuracy in bookkeeping by learning from the user's previous actions and the actions of similar businesses.

- **Receipt Capture**: QBO's Receipt Capture feature uses optical character recognition (OCR) technology to extract data from uploaded receipts and invoices. This reduces manual data entry by automatically filling in the details into the appropriate expense categories, helping users to keep track of spending and simplify tax preparations.

- **Cash Flow Predictor**: QBO offers a cash flow forecasting tool that utilizes AI to predict future cash flows based on past transactions. This feature allows businesses to see projected cash inflows and outflows, helping them plan and manage their finances more effectively.

- **Invoice Automation**: QuickBooks Online automates the invoicing process, which includes creating, sending, and tracking invoices. AI enhances this process by learning from past invoicing behaviours to suggest invoice recipients and due dates, improving the efficiency of accounts receivable processes.

- **Tax Classification**: AI in QBO helps classify transactions for tax purposes, suggesting the tax categories that transactions should be filed under based on the learned behaviour and common practices. This assists businesses in staying compliant with tax obligations with less manual intervention.

- **Anomaly Detection**: QuickBooks uses AI to detect anomalies or unusual patterns in financial data that might indicate errors or potential fraudulent activity. This feature helps ensure the accuracy and security of financial information by alerting users to any irregularities.

- **Personalized Insights and Recommendations**: QBO provides personalized business insights and financial recommendations driven by AI. These insights are tailored to the business's performance and market trends, offering valuable guidance for decision-making.

These AI-driven features represent QuickBooks Online's commitment to leveraging advanced technology to streamline accounting tasks, enhance data accuracy, and provide actionable insights for businesses.

To access and utilize these features for better customer insights, try the following steps:

Step 1: Log in to QuickBooks Online

- **Access QuickBooks Online**: Visit the QuickBooks Online website and log in using your credentials. If you don't have an account, you'll need to sign up and choose the appropriate subscription plan for your business needs.

Step 2: Automated Transaction Categorization

- **Navigate to the Banking Tab**: Once logged in, click on the "Transactions >Bank Transactions" tab from the left-hand menu.

- **Review Transactions**: You'll see your connected bank accounts and the transactions that have been pulled in.
- **Categorize Transactions**: QuickBooks will suggest categories based on its learning from your previous categorization. Review and confirm these suggestions to help the system learn and improve its accuracy.

Step 3: Receipt Capture

- **Go to the Receipts Tab**: Find and click on the "Receipts" option in the "Transactions" left-hand menu.

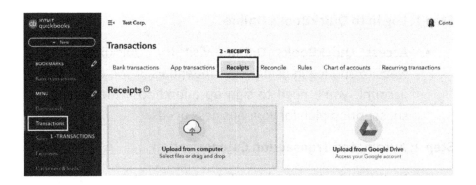

- **Upload a Receipt**: You can drag and drop receipts or click to upload them manually.
- **Review Extracted Data**: Once uploaded, QBO uses OCR to extract data from the receipt. Check and confirm the accuracy of the extracted information, such as the vendor, date, and amount, then save.

Step 4: Cash Flow Predictor

- **Access Cash Flow**: In the dashboard or home screen, look for the "Cash Flow" feature.
- **Review Projections**: The tool provides visual cash flow forecasts based on past transactions. Use this feature to plan for future expenses and incomes.

Step 5: Invoice Automation

- **Navigate to Invoices**: Click on the "Invoices" tab from the sidebar.
- **Create an Invoice**: Select "New Invoice" and fill in the necessary details. QuickBooks will suggest entries like recipient and payment terms based on historical data.
- **Send and Track**: Send the invoice directly from QBO and use the platform to track when it is opened by the recipient.

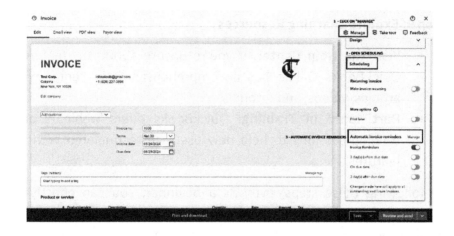

Step 6: Tax Classification

- **Review Transactions for Tax**: As you categorize your transactions, QuickBooks will suggest tax categories. Regularly review and confirm these to ensure accuracy for tax reporting.
- **Prepare for Tax Time**: Use the "Taxes" tab to review your sales tax and other tax categories throughout the year to stay prepared for tax submissions.

Step 7: Anomaly Detection

- **Monitor Alerts**: QBO will automatically notify you of any anomalies or unusual patterns in your account activities. Pay attention to any alerts and review the related transactions.
- **Investigate and Resolve**: If an anomaly is detected, investigate the cause and make necessary corrections to keep your financial records accurate.

Step 8: Personalized Insights and Recommendations

- **Check the Dashboard**: Regularly visit your QBO dashboard, which provides personalized business insights and financial advice.
- **Implement Suggestions**: Use the insights provided by QBO to make informed decisions about your business operations.

Step 9: Explore Learning Resources

- **Visit the Help Center**: If you're unsure about any features, QuickBooks Online has a comprehensive help center with articles, videos, and tutorials.
- **Participate in Training**: QuickBooks offers webinars and training sessions to help new users get acquainted with its features.

By following these steps, even as a beginner, you can effectively leverage the AI capabilities in QuickBooks Online to streamline your business accounting processes, enhance financial decision-making, and maintain accurate records.

Simplifying Tasks: Automated Emails and Personalized Customer Communication

Introduction to Automated Communications

Automated communications in QuickBooks Online (QBO) allow you to save time, improve customer engagement, and streamline your business processes. These features enable you to automate emails, reminders, and notifications to keep your customers informed and your business running smoothly. Here's an introduction to automated communications in QuickBooks Online:

Understanding Automated Communications in QBO:

- Automated communications in QBO are designed to help you manage customer interactions, invoicing, payments, and reminders without manual intervention. By setting up automated emails and notifications, you can ensure timely communication with customers, vendors, and employees.

Key Features of Automated Communications:

Email Reminders:

- Automatically send reminders for upcoming invoices, due dates, and overdue payments.

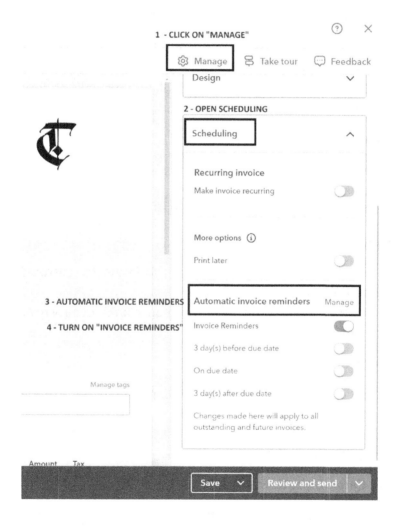

- Improve cash flow by prompting customers to pay on time.

Invoice and Receipt Emails:

- Send automated emails for invoice delivery, payment receipts, and acknowledgments.
- Include payment links, terms, and personalized messages for a professional touch.

Payment Reminders:

- Schedule reminders for outstanding invoices and past-due payments.
- Customize messages and send follow-up emails at designated intervals.

Payment Confirmations:

- Automatically notify customers when their payments are received and processed.
- Provide reassurance and transparency in the payment process.

Estimate and Quote Emails:

- Send estimates, quotes, and proposals to customers via automated emails.
- Include details, terms, and acceptance links for easy review and approval.

Recurring Invoices and Payments:

- Set up recurring invoices for subscription services, memberships, or regular billing.
- Automate payments for subscriptions, installments, or recurring services.

Vendor Communications:

- Automatically send purchase orders, payment confirmations, and vendor statements.
- Streamline communication with vendors for efficient procurement processes.

Employee Notifications:

- Notify employees of payroll updates, timesheet approvals, or benefit changes.
- Automate reminders for expense reporting, time tracking, and HR deadlines.

Benefits of Automated Communications:

Time Savings:

- Reduce manual tasks by automating routine communications.
- Focus on core business activities while QBO handles reminders and notifications.

Improved Cash Flow:

- Prompt payment reminders help accelerate customer payments.
- Reduce late payments and improve overall cash flow for the business.

Enhanced Customer Experience:

- Provide timely updates and information to customers.
- Improve customer satisfaction with professional and personalized communications.

Efficient Operations:

- Streamline invoicing, payments, and vendor interactions with automation.
- Ensure that key tasks and communications are not overlooked or delayed.

Better Organization:

- Stay organized with automated workflows for invoices, estimates, and payments.
- Maintain a clear record of all communications and transactions in QBO.

Increased Productivity:

- Free up staff time from manual follow-ups and reminders.
- Empower employees to focus on strategic tasks and customer relationships.

Setting Up Automated Email Campaigns

As of the last update, QuickBooks Online (QBO) itself does not directly provide functionality for setting up automated email campaigns as it's primarily an accounting software. However, you can integrate QBO with other marketing and email campaign tools like Mailchimp, Constant Contact, or HubSpot using apps available through the QuickBooks App Store or third-party integration platforms like Zapier. Here's a general step-by-step guide on how you might set up automated email campaigns by integrating QBO with an email marketing tool:

Step 1: Choose Your Email Marketing Platform

- **Select a Platform**: Choose an email marketing tool that best fits your business needs (e.g., Mailchimp, Constant Contact, HubSpot).
- **Sign Up/Create an Account**: If you don't already have an account with your chosen platform, sign up and configure your basic account settings.

Step 2: Integrate with QuickBooks Online

- **Visit the QuickBooks App Store**: Go to the QuickBooks App Store and search for your chosen email marketing platform.

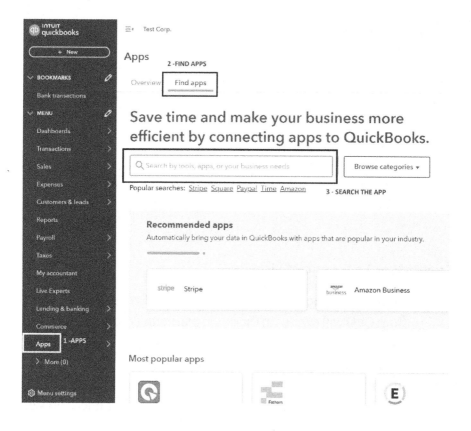

- **Install the App**: Click on the app and select 'Get App Now' to integrate it with your QuickBooks Online account.

- **Authorize Connection**: Follow the prompts to authorize the connection between your QBO account and the email marketing platform.

Step 3: Sync Your Contact List

- **Configure Sync Settings**: Set up how and when your contacts from QBO will sync with the email marketing tool. You may need to map fields from QBO to your email platform to ensure data consistency.
- **Initial Sync**: Perform the initial sync of your contact list from QBO to your email platform. Check for accuracy once the sync is complete.

Step 4: Create Email Campaigns

- **Access the Email Marketing Tool**: Log into your email marketing platform.
- **Design Your Campaign**: Use the tools provided by the platform to create your email content, design your email templates, and set up the campaign flow.
- **Segment Your Audience**: If needed, segment your contacts into different lists or groups based on criteria relevant to your campaign (e.g., customer type, purchase history).

Step 5: Set Up Automation Triggers

- **Define Triggers**: Set up automation rules that trigger emails based on specific actions or time intervals. For example, you might send a welcome email when a new contact is added or a follow-up email after a purchase.

- **Test Your Automation**: Before going live, test your automation triggers to ensure they work as expected.

Step 6: Launch Your Campaign

- **Schedule and Launch**: Schedule your emails and go live. Ensure you have set the appropriate time zones and launch times.
- **Monitor Campaign Performance**: Use the analytics tools provided by the email marketing platform to monitor the performance of your campaigns. Look at metrics like open rates, click rates, and conversions.

Step 7: Maintain and Optimize

- **Regular Updates**: Regularly update your contact list and sync it with QBO.
- **Refine Campaigns**: Based on the campaign performance data, make necessary adjustments to your emails and automation settings to improve effectiveness.

Step 8: Stay Compliant

- **Ensure Compliance**: Make sure your email campaigns comply with email marketing laws and regulations like GDPR, CAN-SPAM, or CASL depending on your location.

This integration can help you enhance customer engagement and drive business growth, but it's only a piece of the puzzle. Segmenting your customer base effectively is also necessary for delivering targeted and personalized communications that resonate with your audience.

Here are some practical tips for segmenting your customer base to enhance the effectiveness of your email campaigns:

1. Use Demographic Data

- **Basics First**: Start with basic demographic data such as age, gender, location, and occupation. This information can be collected during account sign-ups or purchases and provides a foundational way to customize your messaging.
- **Advanced Demographics**: Consider more nuanced demographic factors like marital status, education level, or household income, if relevant to your product or service.

2. Analyze Purchase History

- **Frequency and Recency**: Segment customers based on how often and how recently they have purchased. Target frequent and recent buyers differently from those who purchase sporadically.
- **Purchase Type and Amount**: Look at what types of products customers are buying and the average transaction value. Tailor your communications to promote products similar to what they have bought in the past.

3. Leverage Behavioral Data

- **Engagement Level**: Segment based on engagement levels with your past emails, website visits, or app usage. Send different messages to highly engaged users versus those who are less active.
- **User Actions**: Segment users based on actions they've taken, like downloading a white paper, using a certain feature of your service, or abandoning a shopping cart.

4. Utilize Customer Feedback

- **Survey Responses**: Use data from surveys or feedback forms to segment customers based on their preferences, satisfaction levels, or service experiences.

- **Customer Service Interactions**: Segment customers based on their history of interactions with customer support. Those who have had issues might benefit from follow-up emails ensuring their problems were resolved.

5. Consider Psychographic Factors

- **Personal Interests**: Segment your customers by interests or lifestyle choices, which can often be inferred from social media activity or directly asked in user profiles.
- **Values and Attitudes**: Group customers by shared values or attitudes towards particular topics, which can be particularly effective for companies whose brand or products align with specific ethical or social causes.

6. Geographic Segmentation

- **Regional Preferences**: Customize communications based on geographic location to address regional tastes, climate-related needs, or local events.
- **Local vs. Global**: Distinguish between local customers and those who are national or international, especially if your product delivery or service provision varies by distance.

7. Lifecycle Stages

- **Customer Lifecycle**: Segment customers based on their lifecycle stage—new, active, at-risk, or inactive. Tailor communications to re-engage at-risk or inactive customers, and to maintain relationships with active customers.
- **Loyalty Status**: Use loyalty program data to segment customers based on their tier or status, offering exclusive content or promotions to higher tiers.

8. Technology Use

- **Device Type**: Segment based on the devices customers use to interact with your emails or website (e.g., mobile vs desktop users), tailoring the content format accordingly.

- **Software Preferences**: If applicable, segment based on the type of software or platforms your customers prefer, which can be particularly relevant in B2B communications.

9. Subscription Preferences

- **Content Type**: Pay attention to what types of content your subscribers consume and segment based on preferences for specific topics or formats.
- **Frequency Preferences**: Offer options for how often subscribers receive emails and segment communication strategies based on these preferences.

Effective segmentation allows you to tailor your marketing strategies more precisely and can significantly enhance the effectiveness of your communications by ensuring relevance to each segment of your customer base. This approach not only improves customer engagement but also drives higher conversion rates and customer loyalty.

Integrating with Email Marketing Tools

Integrating QuickBooks Online (QBO) with email marketing tools allows you to streamline your marketing efforts, improve customer communication, and automate campaigns seamlessly. By connecting QBO with popular email marketing platforms, you can synchronize customer data, send targeted emails, and track campaign performance. Here's a guide on how to integrate QBO with email marketing tools:

Benefits of Integrating QBO with Email Marketing Tools:

- **Synchronize Customer Data:** Automatically import customer information from QBO to your email marketing platform.
- **Targeted Email Campaigns:** Segment customers based on purchase history, preferences, or demographics for personalized campaigns.

- **Automated Follow-Ups:** Send automated emails for invoice reminders, promotions, or customer feedback.
- **Improved Efficiency:** Save time by eliminating manual data entry and automating email processes.
- **Track Campaign Performance:** Monitor open rates, click-through rates, and conversions to optimize marketing strategies.

Popular Email Marketing Platforms Compatible with QBO:

Mailchimp:

- Connect Mailchimp with QBO to sync customer data, create targeted campaigns, and track results.
- Easily import customer lists, design email templates, and schedule automated emails.

Constant Contact:

- Integrate Constant Contact to streamline email marketing campaigns with QBO.

- Import contacts, send newsletters, and track engagement for better customer communication.

HubSpot:

- Sync HubSpot with QBO to manage customer relationships, email campaigns, and lead generation.
- Create workflows, segment contacts, and track interactions for personalized communication.

Zoho Campaigns:

- Connect Zoho Campaigns to QBO for email marketing automation and lead nurturing.
- Import customer data, design responsive emails, and analyze campaign performance.

ActiveCampaign:

- Integrate ActiveCampaign with QBO for targeted email marketing and customer engagement.
- Automate email sequences, segment contacts, and measure campaign success.

Steps to Integrate QBO with Email Marketing Tools:

Select Your Email Marketing Platform:

- Choose a compatible email marketing platform that meets your business needs.
- Sign up for an account or log in to your existing account.

Enable Integration in QBO:

- Log in to your QuickBooks Online account.
- Navigate to the "Apps" or "Integrations" section (depending on your version).

Search for Your Email Marketing Tool:

- Use the search function to find your preferred email marketing platform.
- Click on the tool's icon or name to begin the integration process.

Authorize Access:

- Follow the prompts to authorize QBO to connect with your email marketing account.
- Enter your email marketing platform's login credentials to establish the connection.

Enhancing Efficiency: AI-Powered Financial Operations

AI-Enhanced Bookkeeping

Automated transaction categorization in QuickBooks Online (QBO) is a powerful feature that uses artificial intelligence (AI) and machine learning to automatically assign categories to your transactions. This saves time, reduces errors, and helps keep your financial records organized. Here's how automated transaction categorization works in QBO:

Key Features:

AI-Powered Categorization:

- QBO's AI algorithms analyze your transaction history and learn from your categorization patterns.
- It uses this information to automatically categorize new transactions based on similarities with past entries.

Suggested Categories:

- When you review new transactions, QBO suggests categories based on its analysis.
- You can accept these suggestions, modify them, or create rules for future transactions.

Adaptive Learning:

- The AI continuously learns from your corrections and adjustments.
- Over time, it becomes more accurate in categorizing transactions according to your business needs.

Custom Rules:

- Create custom rules for specific vendors, payees, or transaction types.
- QBO will apply these rules to automatically categorize future transactions that match the criteria.

Bank Rules Integration:

- Bank rules work in tandem with AI categorization.
- You can set up bank rules to automatically categorize transactions based on conditions you define.

Benefits:

Time Savings:

- Eliminates the need for manual categorization of each transaction.
- Saves time and effort, especially for businesses with a large volume of transactions.

Reduced Errors:

- Minimizes human errors associated with manual data entry and categorization.
- Improves the accuracy of financial reports and tax filings.

Consistency:

- Ensures consistency in categorizing similar transactions across different periods.
- Maintains a standardized approach to organizing financial data.

Efficiency in Reporting:

- Generates accurate and detailed financial reports with properly categorized transactions.
- Allows for easier analysis of spending patterns, income sources, and budgeting.

Ease of Use:

- Simplifies the bookkeeping process for users, especially those without extensive accounting knowledge.
- Offers a user-friendly interface for reviewing and approving suggested categories.

How to Use Automated Transaction Categorization:

Review Transactions:

- When new transactions are imported into QBO, they appear in the "For Review" tab.
- Navigate to the Banking or Transactions tab to access these transactions.

Suggested Categories:

- QBO suggests categories for each transaction based on its analysis.
- Review the suggestions and make any necessary adjustments.

Accept or Modify Categories:

- Accept the suggested category by clicking on it if it's correct.
- To modify, click on the category field and choose the appropriate category from the dropdown menu.

Create Rules (Optional):

- For recurring transactions with specific patterns, create rules to automate categorization.
- Click on "Create Rule" to set conditions such as vendor name, amount range, or transaction type.

Apply Bank Rules:

- If you have set up bank rules, QBO will automatically categorize transactions that match the rule criteria.
- Ensure that bank rules are accurately configured to avoid miscategorization.

Review and Adjust Regularly:

- Periodically review the categorization of transactions, especially for new vendors or unusual expenses.
- Make corrections or adjustments to improve accuracy over time.

Monitor Learning Progress:

- QBO's AI continues to learn from your corrections and adjustments.
- Over time, it becomes more accurate in categorizing transactions based on your preferences.

Receipt Capture and Data Extraction:

Receipt capture and data extraction in QuickBooks Online (QBO) allows you to easily record expenses by capturing receipt images and extracting key information. This feature utilizes AI technology to streamline the process of entering expense details, saving you time and reducing manual data entry errors. Here's how receipt capture and data extraction work in QBO:

Key Features:

Mobile Receipt Capture:

- Use the QuickBooks mobile app to capture receipt images using your smartphone or tablet.
- Snap photos of paper receipts, invoices, or bills on the go for easy expense tracking.

Upload Receipt Images:

- Alternatively, upload digital receipt images directly to QBO from your computer or device.
- Drag and drop files or browse your computer to select receipt images for upload.

AI-Powered Data Extraction:

- QuickBooks uses AI technology to extract key details from receipt images.
- Automatically captures information such as vendor name, date, amount, and transaction type.

Transaction Matching:

- Matches extracted data from receipts to existing transactions or creates new ones.
- Links receipt images to corresponding expenses for easy reference and auditing.

Digital Storage and Organization:

- Stores receipt images securely in QBO, eliminating the need for paper storage.
- Organizes receipts by date, vendor, or expense category for quick retrieval.

Integration with Expenses:

- Seamlessly integrates captured receipts with your expense transactions in QBO.
- Automatically records expense details, including vendor, amount, and category.

Benefits:

Effortless Expense Tracking:

- Simplifies the process of recording expenses by capturing receipt images.
- Eliminates the need for manual data entry, saving time and reducing errors.

Improved Accuracy:

- AI technology ensures accurate extraction of vendor names, dates, and amounts.
- Minimizes the risk of transcription errors associated with manual entry.

Real-Time Expense Updates:

- Instantly updates your expense transactions with captured receipt details.
- Provides up-to-date financial records for better decision-making.

Paperless Documentation:

- Reduces paper clutter by storing receipt images digitally in QBO.
- Access and review receipts anytime, anywhere, without the need for physical copies.

Audit Trail and Compliance:

- Maintains a clear audit trail by linking receipt images to corresponding expenses.
- Ensures compliance with record-keeping requirements for tax and financial reporting.

Convenience and Accessibility:

- Access receipt images and expense details from any device with internet access.
- Conveniently manage expenses while on the go without the need for paper receipts.

Cash Flow Management

Cash flow management in QuickBooks Online (QBO) helps businesses monitor, analyze, and optimize their cash flow to ensure financial stability and growth. With features for forecasting, tracking, and planning, QBO provides valuable insights into the inflow and outflow of cash. Here's a guide to cash flow management in QuickBooks Online:

Key Features:

Cash Flow Forecasting:

- QBO provides AI-powered cash flow forecasts based on historical data and upcoming transactions.
- Predicts future cash inflows and outflows to help businesses plan ahead.

Bank and Credit Card Feeds:

- Connect bank and credit card accounts to QBO to automatically import transactions.
- Keeps cash flow information up to date and accurate.

Expense Tracking:

- Record and categorize expenses in QBO to track where money is being spent.
- Helps identify areas where expenses can be reduced or optimized.

Invoice Management:

- Create and send invoices directly from QBO to customers.
- Tracks invoice due dates and expected payment dates for cash flow planning.

Bill Payments:

- Schedule and pay bills within QBO to manage outgoing payments.

- Tracks upcoming bills and due dates to avoid late payments.

Reporting and Analytics:

- Generate cash flow reports, profit and loss statements, and balance sheets.
- Provides insights into cash flow trends, patterns, and potential issues.

Benefits:

Improved Financial Planning:

- Enables businesses to forecast future cash needs and plan accordingly.
- Helps prevent cash shortages and ensures funds are available for expenses.

Optimized Cash Flow:

- Identifies opportunities to speed up receivables and delay payables for better cash flow.
- Helps balance cash inflows and outflows to maintain liquidity.

Timely Payments:

- Reminds businesses of upcoming bill payments and invoice due dates.
- Avoids late fees and maintains positive relationships with vendors and creditors.

Better Decision Making:

- Provides data-driven insights for strategic decision-making.
- Helps prioritize investments, expenses, and revenue-generating activities.

Reduced Financial Stress:

- By having a clear view of cash flow, businesses can reduce financial uncertainty and stress.
- Improves overall financial management and stability.

How to Manage Cash Flow in QBO:

Set Up Bank Feeds:

- Connect your bank and credit card accounts to QBO for automatic transaction syncing.
- Ensures that cash flow information is up-to-date and accurate.

Review Cash Flow Forecast:

- Access the Cash Flow Forecast feature in QBO.
- Review predicted cash inflows and outflows for upcoming periods.

Monitor Receivables and Payables:

- Track outstanding customer invoices and expected payment dates.
- Review upcoming bills and their due dates for timely payments.

Create Cash Flow Reports:

- Generate cash flow reports in QBO to analyze historical trends and patterns.
- Use insights to make informed decisions about spending, investments, and savings.

Setting up Automated Payment Reminders

Setting up automated payment reminders in QBO is an effective way to manage your cash flow by ensuring timely payments from your customers. Here's how you can set up automated payment reminders:

Step 1: Log in to QuickBooks Online

- **Access Your Account**: Open your web browser, go to the QuickBooks Online login page, and enter your credentials to log in.

Step 2: Navigate to the Invoicing Features

- **Go to Invoices**: From the dashboard or the sidebar menu, click on "Sales" and then select "Invoices" to view your list of invoices.

Step 3: Set Up Reminder Preferences

- **Access Invoice Settings**: In the Invoices section, look for a gear icon, settings, or similar options to find invoicing features.

- **Find Reminder Settings**: Look for an option labeled "Reminders" or "Automation" where you can manage communication settings.

Step 4: Configure Automated Reminders

- **Enable Reminders**: If not already enabled, turn on the automated reminders feature.
- **Customize Reminder Rules**:
  - **Timing**: Decide how many days before or after an invoice due date you want to send the reminders. Common settings are 7 days before, 1 day before, and 1 day after the due date.
  - **Frequency**: Set how frequently the reminders should be sent if the invoice remains unpaid. For example, you might want to send a reminder every week after the due date.
- **Personalize Reminder Messages**: Customize the email template for reminders. Keep the tone polite and professional. Clearly state the invoice details, due date, and how they can make a payment. You may also include a link directly to the invoice or payment portal.

Step 5: Apply Reminder Settings to Invoices

- **Select Invoices**: Apply the reminder settings either to all invoices by default or select specific invoices for which you want to enable reminders.
- **Review Settings**: Ensure that the reminders are correctly set up for each chosen invoice.

Step 6: Automate Late Fees (Optional)

- **Set Up Late Fees**: If you want to apply late fees for overdue payments, go back to the invoicing settings.
- **Configure Late Fee Rules**: Define the amount or percentage of the late fee and when it should be applied (e.g., 2% of the invoice amount 10 days after the due date).

Step 7: Monitor and Adjust

- **Keep Track of Reminders**: Regularly check the status of sent reminders and the response or payment status from customers.
- **Adjust Settings as Needed**: Based on customer feedback or payment trends, adjust reminder timings or messages to optimize their effectiveness.

Step 8: Communicate with Your Customers

- **Inform Your Customers**: When you begin using automated reminders, inform your customers about this change. Explain that this system is in place to streamline communication and ensure timely services.

Step 9: Evaluate Cash Flow Impact

- **Review Cash Flow Changes**: After a few billing cycles with automated reminders, evaluate their impact on your cash flow.
- **Make Necessary Adjustments**: If you see improvements, consider further optimizations. If not, review your reminder strategies and possibly seek customer feedback for insights.

By setting up automated payment reminders in QuickBooks Online, you can reduce the administrative burden of chasing payments and improve your cash flow management. This not only helps maintain a healthy business operation but also reinforces professional communication with your customers.

Reporting and Insights

Custom report generation in QuickBooks Online (QBO) allows businesses to create personalized reports tailored to their specific needs. These reports can provide detailed insights into various aspects of the business, including finances, sales, expenses, and more. Here's a guide on how to create custom reports in QuickBooks Online:

Accessing Reports in QuickBooks Online:

- Log in to your QuickBooks Online account.
- Navigate to the left-hand menu and select "Reports."

Selecting a Report:

- In the Reports menu, you'll see a list of standard reports grouped by category.
- Browse the categories such as "Business Overview," "Sales and Customers," "Expenses and Vendors," etc.

Creating a Custom Report:

Choose a Report to Customize:

- Select a standard report that closely matches the information you need.
- Click on the report name to open it.

Customize Report Settings:

- Once the report is open, look for the "Customize" button at the top-right corner.
- Click on "Customize" to access the customization options.

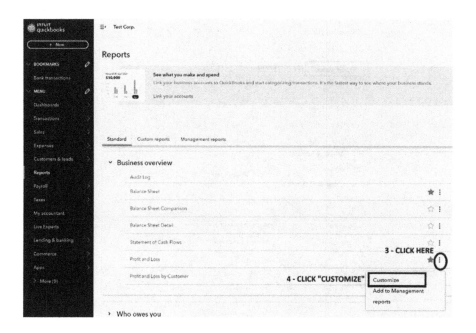

Report Period:

- Set the date range for the report using the "Report period" drop-down menu.
- Choose a preset range or set a custom date range.

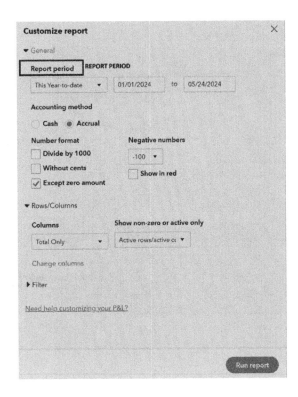

Columns and Rows:

- Customize the columns and rows of the report to display specific data.
- Click on the "Rows/Columns" button to add, remove, or rearrange columns.

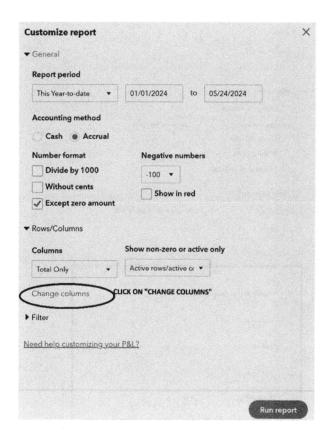

Filters:

- Apply filters to narrow down the data included in the report.
- Click on the "Filter" button to add filter criteria such as account, customer, class, etc.

Header/Footer:

- Customize the report header and footer with your business name, logo, and other details.

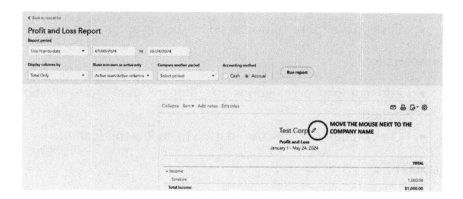

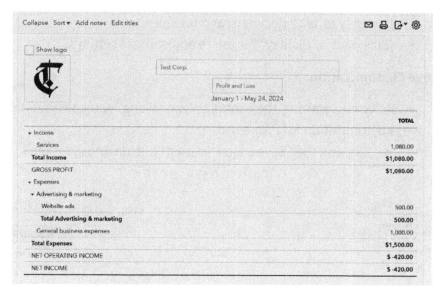

- Click on the "Header/Footer" button to edit these sections.

Data Layout:

- Adjust the data layout to group information by specific criteria.

- Click on the "Rows/Columns" button and select "Change columns" to modify the layout.

Sorting:

- Arrange the data in the report in a specific order.
- Click on the "Sort" button to select sorting options for columns.

Comparison:

- Add comparison columns to compare data from different periods.
- Click on the "Comparison" button to enable this feature.

Display:

- Customize how the data is displayed in the report, such as currency format, decimals, and totals.
- Click on the "Display" button to adjust these settings.

Save Customization:

- After customizing the report to your liking, you can save the customization for future use.
  - Click on the "Save customization" button and give your custom report a name.

CONCLUSION

As you turn the final page of this guide, you stand at the threshold of a new step in your business journey; financial clarity and control are now easier, thanks to QuickBooks Online. Take your time and go through this manual as many times as you need to master one of the most powerful tools for business finance management.

With the knowledge and skills you've gained from this book, you are well-equipped to digitally navigate the complexities of financial management with confidence and precision. Embrace the capabilities of digitized accounting and continue to explore QBO's features and updates. Each function is designed to enhance your understanding of your business's financial health, allowing you to forecast future needs and adjust your strategies accordingly. Your proactive engagement with this tool will keep your operations agile and responsive to the ever-changing commercial landscape.

Challenges may arise as with any other venture or change, but with a robust tool like QuickBooks Online at your disposal, you have the resources to meet them head-on. Stay curious, remain vigilant, and keep learning. Every piece of financial data you manage efficiently is a stepping stone towards greater success.

So, go forth with the assurance that you can and will thrive. Here's to your success and the endless possibilities that lie ahead.

Made in the USA
Las Vegas, NV
28 October 2024

10648869R00125